FROZEN ASSETS

First presented by the Royal Shakespeare Company in January 1978 as part of their highly successful Warehouse season, **Frozen Assets** is 'a modern morality play . . . The hero is Buddy, a Borstal boy on the run after accidentally killing a warder: a victim of chance who needs help and counsel but discovers for himself the predatory nature of the world.' (John Peter, *Sunday Times*)

'Barrie Keeffe, who gave us some searing impressions of juvenile rebelliousness recently, has detached himself from his material and begun the long climb demanded of the true artist. *A Mad World My Masters,* a hilarious Jonsonian romp, was the first step in the new direction. **Frozen Assets** is a further milestone.' (France Marcus, *Sunday Telegraph*)

'. . . contains sustained stretches of flashingly truthful dialogue and splendidly imagined comic scenes.' (Irving Wardle, *The Times*)

'. . . a vivid picaresque sweep through our crooked social strata . . . in which Keeffe ironically counterpoints the comic realities of knavery at every level of modern life . . . the play is an affirmation of energy and a possibly desperate plea for decency and concern.' (Tony Coult, *Plays and Players*) *in the same series*

EAST-WEST & IS UNCLE JACK A CONFORMIST?
by Andrey Amalrik

A-A-AMERICA! & STONE
by Edward Bond

FIGHT FOR SHELTON BAR
Victoria Theatre, Stoke-on-Trent
edited by Peter Cheeseman

POOR TOM & TINA
by David Cregan

WRECKERS
by David Edgar

A MAD WORLD, MY MASTERS
by Barrie Keeffe

LAVENDER BLUE & NOLI ME TANGERE
by John Mackendrick

AMERICAN BUFFALO, SEXUAL PERVERSITY IN CHICAGO & DUCK VARIATIONS
by David Mamet

STRAWBERRY FIELDS
by Stephen Poliakoff

BRIMSTONE AND TREACLE
by Dennis Potter

CLASS ENEMY
by Nigel Williams

FROZEN ASSETS

BARRIE KEEFFE

A Methuen New Theatrescript
Eyre Methuen · London

To Verity

First published in 1978 by Eyre Methuen Ltd, 11 New Fetter Lane,
London EC4P 4EE

Printed in Great Britain by Expression Printers Ltd, London

ISBN 0 413 45730 3

Frozen Assets was commissioned and first performed by the Royal Shakespeare Company at the Warehouse Theatre, London on January 9th 1978 with the following cast:

BUDDY	Allan Hendrick
SCREW	David Waller
AUNTIE CONNIE	Ruby Head
PAM	Marjorie Bland
RONNIE	David Howey
FRANK	Martin Read
JOAN	Marilyn Goldsworthy
AL	Fred Molina
PRIEST	John Nettles
DAVE	Kevin O'Shea
SAMMY	Clyde Pollitt
EDNA	Denyse Alexander
HENRY	Martin Read
LORD PLAISTOW	David Waller
PETER	John Nettles

Directed by Barry Kyle
Designed by Sally Gardner

ACT ONE

Music before play: The Band's 'Christmas Must Be Tonight', from the album Islands.
Empty stage, cold winter light. A dirty plank set stage right. A dead duck set centre upstage. And a football.
Music fades. Sound of wind. BUDDY *enters, shivering with the cold. About 17, with short Borstal hair and Borstal uniform: blue and white pin-striped shirt, plimsolls and jeans too short in the leg and too large at the waist; he has tightened the waistband with large safety pins.*
He shivers, rubs his shoulders to keep warm.

BUDDY: Shit. Ball in the river. Stuck on the ice. If it was a goal everytime someone kicked it in the river, we'd run up a landslide against them village poufs.

He pauses and wonders how to get the ball. Then he dashes off and returns immediately with a spiked pole.

This's what'll get it. They said I could play football today.

He gets the plank and rests it across the imaginary river towards the football.

They promised me. I even got changed, and put on the linseed oil – on me legs. I was all ready to go, then Jamie said his bugger of a leg was better and that he was playing after all. So I put me clothes back on and went behind the goal. I have to get the ball everytime one of them village poufs misses the goal and it comes out here, on the outside. I'm doing more jumping about than our goalie.

He gingerly balances on the plank with the spike to try and reach the ball. He cannot quite reach it. Instead he spikes the dead duck. he picks up the duck.

Blimey. Copped it.

VOICE: Clark. Clark!

BUDDY *is fascinated by the duck as* SCREW, *the Borstal warder, enters.*

SCREW: Clark, what are you doing out here?

BUDDY: It's a dead duck.

SCREW: Did you kill it?

BUDDY: Kill it? Me? No, 'course not, 'course I never.

SCREW: I'm very glad to hear it. (*Take duck.*) Little duck out for a walk. Not out to get spliced with a spike by the likes of you.

BUDDY: I know. (*Exaggerated sympathy.*) Poor little duck.

SCREW: Are you taking the piss?

BUDDY: Nar –

SCREW: A lot of people think it's a bit peculiar – a man my age liking ducks.

BUDDY: I like them and all.

SCREW: Ducks never hurt no-one. Give them a pond and a few crusts of bread and they're happy.

BUDDY: This one don't look too happy

SCREW: It's dead, isn't it! Some people would eat that. Bung it in a stew or something. When I became fond of ducks, I turned vegetarian.

BUDDY: Did you?

SCREW: I would have gone macro-biotic, but me wife put her foot down.

BUDDY: Hard cheese.

SCREW: That's what made her fed up – the cheese all the time, every meal.

BUDDY: Better than eating ducks.

SCREW: Don't know how people can do it. It's a tufted scaup.

BUDDY: A what?

SCREW: Name of the duck. Fresh water variety. You can learn a lot of things from ducks. Like for instance . . . You sure you're not taking the piss?

BUDDY: No, I'm very interested. It's just that I don't know much about them.

SCREW: See, he's in his water plumage. In the winter it's black and white. In the summer he'd be brown and white. If you're not sure whether it's winter or summer, take a look at a tufted scaup and Bob's Your Uncle.

BUDDY: Thanks for the tip. Poor little thing – lovely looking.

SCREW: Should be in Iceland or somewhere like that, this time of year. A fox must have got it. Or them vicious little bleeders in there. You're Clark aren't you?

BUDDY: Yeah.

SCREW: I thought so. What are you doing outside the permitted perimeter?

BUDDY: I come to get the ball, didn't I. It come out.

SCREW: Better throw it back over the fence and get round there inside ourselves.

BUDDY,*on the plank, reaches for the ball, holding the* SCREW's *hand so that he can stretch further. He retrieves the ball and then throws it off stage.*

BUDDY: They said I could play.

SCREW: In the prestige Christmas match against the village?

BUDDY: But Jamie played, because his leg's better. Smells nice outside here. Better than in there.

SCREW: You're not like a young lag, Clark. I see no deep seated villainy in your eyes. I've got one your age myself.

BUDDY: I only nicked a car.

SCREW: And they put you in there?

BUDDY: I did it a few times. Driving cars is my hobby.

SCREW: I see.

BUDDY: Pity I ain't got one.

SCREW: That would be a bit of a handicap. How long to go?

BUDDY: Four weeks and I'm out.

SCREW: Keep out of trouble.

BUDDY: I am.

SCREW: Don't let no-one rile you. Fuck up your good behaviour.

BUDDY: I ain't been in no trouble since I've been in the nick.

SCREW: Think what it's like out here, out here in the country. Breathe it in. Keep it in your lungs so you can remember in there – amid all the stench of latrines and shit and stale spunk. Remember the smell and the goodness of the world outside the prison. Remember and you will keep out of trouble.

BUDDY: Yes.

SCREW: What can you smell, Clark?

BUDDY (*deep breath, then*): Trees . . . and a bonfire somewhere. Tree smoke . . . cut grass under the snow . . . animal smells . . . and hay burning? I liked October, when they burned the hay in the evenings in the fields.

SCREW: God honest smells, every one of them. You're shivering.

BUDDY: They wouldn't let me put on me jumper, because it's sport.

SCREW: They're barbaric, some of them, even if I do say it myself. Keep this duck out of their sight. I'll bury it later. See down river? Down stream, by the village. Kids skating on the river. All right, that, eh? When you're free, take up skating and duck watching. Keep you out of trouble.

BUDDY: I will. (*Slight pause.*) There was a duck pond in the park.

SCREW: Eh?

BUDDY: In the park, near home. This man, he fed them. He was mad. They said he was mad. We all walked faster when we passed him in the street. But no need to run – he only had one leg. The other one was wooden.

SCREW: Only having one leg don't mean you're mad. It's like saying if you've only got one arm you're deaf.

BUDDY: Point was: when he walked along, he always kept his hand over his head, like this. (*Places right arm across head.*) So God didn't get his angels to shit on his head.

SCREW: God's got more important things to do with his angels.

BUDDY: And everyone was scared of the madman in the park. I've got toothache.

SCREW: Seen the dentist?

BUDDY: He's off until after Christmas.

SCREW: Bloody typical. Your face looks swollen. Ridiculous in this day and age going round with toothache. I'll give him a phone up for you – get him in to look at you this afternoon.

BUDDY: O tar.

During these last few lines, BUDDY *has picked up the plank, holding it dead centre and horizontal to the ground. The* SCREW *has picked up the spike, its point pointing into his stomach and the other end waist high.* BUDDY *turns with the plank; the end hammers the spike into the* SCREW's *stomach. The* SCREW *falls to his knees.*

BUDDY: O Jesus Christ!

SCREW: You stupid cunt.

BUDDY: You're all bleeding and bloody.

SCREW: Get it out! Get it out, you daft prat.

BUDDY: Accident, only accident, honest. Didn't mean, didn't mean. You're nice to me.

SCREW: Get this fucking thing out of my guts. Errrrr.

BUDDY *tugs at spike. It snaps in his hands.*

Help, help me. Me whistle, sound the alarm, blow me whistle.

BUDDY (*shouts*). Help, help!

SCREW: Whistle, whistle!

BUDDY: Where, where?

SCREW: Pocket, pocket!

BUDDY: Move over a bit then so that I can –

SCREW: You fucking daft bleeder.

BUDDY: Move over and –

SCREW: You sure you never spiked that duck?

BUDDY: I promise I never.

SCREW: Me whistle.

The SCREW *moves over to enable* BUDDY *to get his hand in to take the whistle.* BUDDY *blows it – but instead of being a prison whistle it's a duck warbler. He goes to the* SCREW's *other pocket. The* SCREW *lies motionless. He is dead.*

BUDDY: Got it, get help now. I was only getting the ball. You'll be all right, matey. You won't miss the Christmas carol service. I'll bury the duck and –

He goes to blow the whistle, but becomes aware of the sudden stiffness of the SCREW. *He prods the* SCREW *with his foot. The* SCREW's *arms fall flat.*

O Jesus Christ! O Jesus. You're all right, really you are. You're just a little bit tired. All this fresh air. A bit upset 'cause of the duck getting killed. Having a little rest are you, a little rest? Aren't you. PLEASE PLEASE. PLEASE SAY YES.

He looks at the motionless corpse.

Accident, didn't mean . . . I'm a reformed person. I . . . O . . . Jesus, Jesus, Jesus.

He blows frenziedly on the whistle again and again.
Then, several sirens sound off.
BUDDY *panics. He goes to dash off, taking the whistle. But he runs back to the duck and takes it as the sirens and alarms reach a crescendo.*
Blackout. Yellow searchlights comb the auditorium and the sirens continue. Then silence.
A misty evening light. The wreck of a car, wheelless, doorless and rusty.
Enter BUDDY, *breathless. He leans panting on the wreck of the car.*

BUDDY: I can still hear the bells ringing in me ears. Like loud pub music – the Boomtown Rats and the Pistols and . . . When you're too near the speaker. And in the quiet outside, you don't know whether you can still really hear it or whether it's just a buzzing in your ears.

He breathes deeply. Silence. Then a

torch on his face and enter CONNIE, *scruffy, about 60.*

CONNIE: Anyone follow you?

BUDDY: Nar.

CONNIE: Dogs?

BUDDY: Nar.

CONNIE: I knew you'd come here. That's why I come here. 'Cause I knew you'd come here. You was mad to come here.

BUDDY: How did you know I was out?

CONNIE: I heard. Someone told me. I was in the boozer and someone told me. Didn't know it would be you. I come down here and stood watching you and I thought: 'That's my fucking nephew'. I nearly went back to the pub.

BUDDY: It was good of you to come.

CONNIE: Everyone who breaks out of the prison comes here. For a car. Breakers' yard! Stupid place to come for a motor.

BUDDY: Got to get out of the area, I've got to.

CONNIE: Don't tell me what you've done. I heard. I said: 'God help the poor little sod when they find him'.

BUDDY: I got you a duck.

CONNIE: A what?

BUDDY: A duck. For you.

CONNIE: Thank you, Buddy. That's very nice of you.

BUDDY: Uncle Harold –

CONNIE: Your Uncle Harold's dead.

BUDDY: I never knew that.

CONNIE: Didn't your mum write and tell you? Broke his heart when his breathing got so bad. He come here every day.

BUDDY: I know.

CONNIE: Must have been for . . . fifty years. He loved it here. The yard – it was the love of his life.

BUDDY: Yeah, I know.

CONNIE: He come down here every day, hell or high water. And at night sometimes. After the pub. To stand here. He said he could hear the horses in the sheds.

BUDDY: He always liked the horses.

CONNIE: Then he came one day, but he couldn't walk from the bus. He couldn't get here. He got on another bus and came home. He was a broken man. I said: 'What's the matter Harold?' He said: 'I ain't got the breath no more. I couldn't walk to the yard.' (*Pause.*) I blame it on them Gold Flake cigarettes. Too strong. He had phlegm on his chest like a hot water bottle. (*Pause.*) I miss him.

BUDDY: I do and all.

CONNIE: That night, I come down here after the funeral. I thought I could hear the horses meself. Mourning for your Uncle Harold. Listen! Wind whistling in the rotting planks of the sheds. Can't you hear it?

BUDDY (*pause, then*): Yeah!

CONNIE: What else can you hear?

BUDDY *agitated, wants to be off.*

Imagine, can't you. Can't you hear the horses?

BUDDY: Oh yeah, O yeah. Can hear them.

CONNIE: What are they doing?

BUDDY: Stamping their hooves. And neighing. And swishing their tails against the walls of the sheds.

CONNIE: You're a lying bleeder. There ain't been a horse here since the war.

BUDDY: I didn't know what to say.

CONNIE: I'm sorry I can't help you, Buddy.

BUDDY: But Auntie Connie! I'm in trouble.

CONNIE: I can't help you, Buddy. They'll be combing the countryside. I can't hide you here. I ain't got a car here except in hundreds of pieces. This is a breaker's yard now.

BUDDY: I'm glad you kept the yard.

CONNIE: You can have wheels or windows or engines. You can take whatever you like, but none of it works if you ain't got a car to put it in. Sorry, boy. (*Pause.*) Funny, miles from anywhere, and the lights of the prison. See them for miles. Even in the mist. Yellow lights in the orchards.

BUDDY *strokes the bonnet of a car.* CONNIE *goes to him.*

Funny, a bloke here this morning come in and asked for a carburettor for a Cortina. 'What model?' I said. He said: 'A green one.' (*They both laugh.*) He never cared about cars like you do.

BUDDY: Yeah, well look where it's got me.

CONNIE: They never come to see me, your family. Even when Harold died, they never come.

BUDDY: They're a bit funny like that.

CONNIE: Should have come and lived out here in the country. Kept you out of trouble. Away from bad influences.

BUDDY: There weren't many country boys in there. Still, too late now.

CONNIE: The alarm bells have stopped ringing.

Silence, they listen.

BUDDY: What will I do?

CONNIE: Keep moving. Get to London. There they'll help you.

BUDDY: I didn't do it on purpose, you know. It was an accident.

CONNIE: Nick a motor from the pub. Half a mile down the road.

BUDDY: All right.

CONNIE: Want a key?

BUDDY: Got a hairclip?

CONNIE: You've learned all that then? When it's over . . . come back here. Could use a man who knows about cars. I'll make you a partner.

BUDDY: All right.

CONNIE: Some clothes. Harold's – in the end shed. Dump the prison clothes somewhere else. Not here. Ssssh . . .

Sound of a car stopping, off. Headlamps on CONNIE. BUDDY *ducks out of sight and crawls off. Dogs bark.*

CONNIE (*calls after* BUDDY): Tell you mother, if she'd have come here, you wouldn't be running like a scared rabbit tonight. Quick, go. And tar for the ducks.

CONNIE *walks towards the headlamps.*

If you bastards don't get off my late husband's property, I'll blow your heads off with a shotgun.

VOICE: Police, missus.

CONNIE: Get a search warrant. Go on, prove it. Show your identity. And I'll have to get me reading glasses.

CONNIE *exits. Blackout.*
Back projection: motorway at night. BUDDY *sits in a car facing the audience.*

BUDDY: Ice on the road, turn into the skids, turn into the skids. Right mouse holes in this bodywork. Fancy having a nice car and letting it fall to bits. But got a radio.

He turns on the radio: Silent Night. Another slide of motorway at night.

Leave the Old Bill tramping round in the slush behind. It'll be closing time before the geezer knows his motor's been nicked then . . . safe. Heart thumping. Nice carol. (*Sings.*) Silent night, Holy night . . . The ones in there, the ones who are alcoholics, they get them off on Jesus. Give them God instead of the Johnny Walker. (*Laughs uncontrollably. Staggers out of car and vomits over bonnet. Pauses.*) Didn't mean it. Didn't mean it. Should have pushed the body in the fucking stream. Tell them it was an accident? What, and have them rattle the cell keys in your mouth? Smash your teeth out? Iron bar up your arsehole? On the fucking run! Ain't like this in Kojak. (*Calms.*) Get home . . . nice cup of tea. Lot of sugar. And this fucking toothache! Tooth stops hurting and everything'll be all right.

Blackout. Police radio tells of suspect on the run.

Lights up on PAM *sitting in an armchair drinking, with a whisky bottle at her foot. An attractive woman, about 28.*

Singing 'Jingle Bells', RONNIE *enters, pulling on a rail of expensive coats – fur and leather – and a truck laden with tv sets, radios, stereos, parcels wrapped in Christmas paper and handbags. He tries on a full-length leather overcoat.*

RONNIE: Well, what do you think?

PAM: All right.

RONNIE: All right? Is that all you can say? Must be worth over a ton for Christ's sake. Hardly been worn, not a crease.

PAM: Yeah. Al phoned. He'll be here with the lorries in half an hour.

RONNIE: Good. I wish you'd leave off that for one night, Pam. Especially tonight. Very big night. Makes me nervous. Christ, I can smell you like a distillery when you get out of the lift, let alone in here.

PAM: It's Christmas.

RONNIE: What about the other three hundred odd nights?

PAM: Practising for Christmas.

RONNIE: Yeah.

He takes out an electronic calculator and begins to evaluate coats. She fingers the parcels.

PAM: Shall I open them?

RONNIE: Nar, leave them. Leave them, will you!

PAM: Might be something I'm after. Some Joy perfume or something. Only sniffing.

RONNIE: Leave them, Pam. I said leave them. (*Grabs her arm.*)

PAM: You're hurting my arm.

RONNIE: Don't make me then. (*He releases her.*)

PAM: You're violent. I don't know why your eyebrows aren't joined together. Like your moustache.

RONNIE: Shut up, will you. I've jumped a digit.

PAM: Remember the wedding? When Al put that underarm hair-remover on his eyebrows. So they didn't join together. For the wedding photos your best man looked like Henry Cooper. Eyes all swollen up and puffy. You did the milkman, didn't you?

RONNIE: Leave off, Pam. You're pissed.

PAM: I know you did him. You bastard. He was a nice man. Everyone here in the flats saying how terrible – and me knowing it was you, you bastard.

RONNIE: Don't get dramatic.

She tops up her glass and goes to the coats. RONNIE *checks his watch.*

Get a move on, Frank, get a move on.

PAM: Nice coat, real fur.

RONNIE: 'Course it's real. No plastic smelling imitation stuff for these tight arsed nobs. Real pig stinking hide and leopard skin. And wardrobes smelling like fucking zoos. Here, try these for size.

PAM: What?

RONNIE (*tosses them at her*): Leather knickers.

PAM: Don't be disgusting, what do you take me for?

RONNIE: Go on!

PAM: Where did you get them?

RONNIE (*produces whip and cracks it*): Yeah!

PAM (*screams and then laughs*): God Almighty, how positively vile. How perverted.

RONNIE: Solicitor's house. In Tudor Avenue. Must be sixty grand. Right posh. There's a lot of fucking money about.

PAM: How perverted.

RONNIE: Leaded windows, carpets full of static. Get an electric shock every-time you touch a door handle. Bath like a Persian shit house. Perverts. Five grand here. We get nearer that apartment in Teneriffe.

PAM: The woman in the greengrocers said you can get a maid to keep the place clean during the out of season for seven quid a month. She said they're everso nice.

RONNIE: We'll have all that.

PAM: I'm everso surprised at the woman in the greengrocer's having one.

RONNIE: Show me anyone who's made a lot of money from nothing and I'll show you a villain.

PAM: I wonder if there's any Joy parfum in them presents? Go on, let me have a look.

Enter FRANK*; suntanned man in an airline uniform.*

FRANK: How are we going?

RONNIE: See for yourself.

FRANK: Hello Pam. These yours? (*He fingers the leather knickers on the chair.*)

PAM (*giggling*): Shall I try them on?

RONNIE: Pam!

PAM: You said –

RONNIE: Shut your hole! Good to see you Frank.

FRANK: Happy Christmas.

RONNIE: It's a great night. have a drink, Frank, have a drink. (*Hands him* PAM's *glass.*)

FRANK: Cheers.

RONNIE: Get the other addresses?

FRANK: Got five. Here. There's a party on at Heathrow, so I'd better not hang about. Those addresses, all in this neighbourhood.

RONNIE (*looks at the list*): Frank – take a colour tele, take a colour tv.

FRANK: Another time. Be in touch.

FRANK *goes and* RONNIE *continues to study the list.*

PAM: They're so dashing them airline pilots.

RONNIE: He's a fucking ticket clerk.

Pause. RONNIE *continues to read the list.* PAM *looks at presents.*

PAM: Don't you feel . . . (*Pause.*) Especially at Christmas?

RONNIE: What?

PAM: Doing it at Christmas?

Pause. RONNIE *lights a cigar slowly.*

RONNIE: Nothing. Feel, nothing.

PAM: All their houses? All twinkling with coloured lights and smelling nice and decorations?

RONNIE: No decorations for this lot. They'll all be in the fucking West Indies. Bastards spending Christmas in paradise. Good old Frank. These five families, be in the air time we detonate them.

PAM (*reads list*): Walnut Close. Raynor Hill. Such nice names, all in huge beautiful gardens I bet. Next Christmas we might be in our apartment in Teneriffe. And you in the Scrubs again.

RONNIE *slaps her face hard at the mention of prison. She tries to turn it into a joke.*

What if when we're in Teneriffe someone robs us?

RONNIE: Never . . . rob . . . your . . . own . . . class.

PAM: Robin Fucking Hood.

RONNIE: Tell Sid to come back here at about three in the morning. There'll be a second shipping. And tell him to lay off the booze till he's dropped it. (*Starts to go, stops.*) And if Smithy rings, ask him where the fuck he's been! (*He exits.*)

PAM, *alone, switches on the radio. 'Away in a Manger'. Gingerly, she tries on the leather knickers, opening her dress to waist height to show them off. She sits and refills the glass.* BUDDY *enters quietly, wearing an old man's raincoat.*
He goes behind PAM *and puts his hands over her eyes.*

PAM: Buddy, Buddy – my darling little brother, it's you!

BUDDY: I waited till Ronnie went and then I come in.

PAM: What are you doing here? And where did you get that thing? Just like that smelly old coat Uncle Harold used to wear.

BUDDY: Parole.

Pause.

PAM: Bit sudden in't it? No warning.

BUDDY: They was very generous, they said, well, seeing it's Christmas, all you that's on good behaviour, go home for a few days. (*He is staring at her leather knickers.*)

PAM: O! A joke . . . (*Takes them off.*) Good to see you.

BUDDY: I went home, but there was no answer.

PAM: Mum's in hospital again.

BUDDY: O, I wondered . . . when?

PAM: Day before yesterday. No. It was Tuesday.

BUDDY: O.

PAM: She'll be all right, just needs another transfusion.

BUDDY: They're getting more often.

PAM: The doctor said that's what'd happen.

BUDDY: Ronnie's busy then.

PAM: Yeah, one day I'll come in this room and be surprised because it's not full of fur coats and colour tellies.

BUDDY: Must have been planning this one. And him on probation and all.

PAM: He can charm the leaves off the trees, my Ronnie can. She was here yesterday, his probation officer, daft cow. That post office job. Grievous bodily harm and all. Probation, his record! He sat on the stereo crying like a baby. Said it was all 'cause he saw his dad beat up his mum when he was a baby in his pram.

PAM and BUDDY: Vivid childhood memory!

PAM: She believed him, lent him some Kleenex.

BUDDY: He's got a lucky one.

PAM: No wonder he needs glasses to watch tv. (*Sees others.*) Teles. He says it himself, he does. It was reading all them fucking psychiatry books in the Scrubs. The bleeder. And they give you eighteen months for a few harmless little motors. There don't seem no justice. (*Pause.*) Take your coat off then. Might have given you something a bit more decent to wear in this weather. In't it bitter.

BUDDY: Bit nippy. Pam, ain't got an Anadin have you?

PAM: Side of your face is all swelled up. Let me look, come here. Looks really painful.

BUDDY: Tooth hurting.

PAM: Here, let me see. Turn round a bit.

His coat falls open. She sees the uniform.

PAM: Buddy, them clothes! Buddy, Buddy, my darling little brother – they haven't let you out on parole (*Pause.*) Don't lie to me. Enough lying in this family.

Pause.

BUDDY: I did a bunk, didn't I.

Pause.

PAM: Over the wall. On the run. With others? You was led astray . . .

BUDDY: Over the wall. On me own. (*Puts his hand over his head.*)

PAM: But darling . . . why? You only had another four weeks. You said in your letter the governor had told you when you was leaving! In four weeks you'd have been out anyway.

BUDDY: I got . . .

Pause.

PAM: What?

BUDDY: Fed up, bit fed up, you know. Frightened, Pam. Shaking, see? Can I have a fag?

PAM: Yeah, here. (*Hands him a cigarette.*) I mean to say, my Ronnie's a bit highly strung and impetuous, but even he has the sense not to break out, not when you've only got a month to go.

BUDDY: And them Anadins?

PAM: In me handbag.

BUDDY *goes to the handbags on the truck.*

No, not that one. I haven't had a chance to go through all them yet. Looks really painful, way it's all swelling up.

BUDDY: It is.

He takes two Anadins and swallows them, washing them down with PAM's *whisky which makes him groan.*

PAM: Then say, say it was the PAIN. Say you didn't know what you was doing because you was delirious with pain and . . . and . . .

BUDDY: Eh?

PAM: Delirious with pain and could you please go back and would they please overlook it. Ronnie'll tell you what to say. Something psychiatric. Why you did it. Then he'll give you a lift back to the prison, after he's burgled the houses in Walnut Close and Tudor Drive.

BUDDY: Pam . . .

Pause. He paces.

PAM: Weren't they waiting for you outside mum's?

BUDDY: Mum weren't there.

PAM: She went into hospital.

BUDDY: Day before yesterday.

PAM: Tuesday.

BUDDY: On Tuesday, yeah.

PAM: For another –

BUDDY: Transfusion.

PAM: – transfusion, you see the doctor said –

BUDDY: Killed this screw.

He begins to shiver.

PAM: And the doctor said she'll have to have more transfusions more often now because the red corpuscles aren't reproducing so fast now that the –

BUDDY: This screw, I killed him.

PAM: I thought that might have something to do with why we can't have a baby, though I don't know how we'd get on in Teneriffe with a baby, though mind you, we haven't got the apartment yet and spending all these hundreds and hundreds of pounds on tests and different treatments and then when we tried to adopt, just on account of Ronnie's records the adoption people said there's thousands of couples who are decent people and can't have kids and so we couldn't even be considered. I haven't got a criminal record.

BUDDY: I murdered this screw.

Silence.

PAM: Buddy, Buddy, you mustn't murder screws, not screws. That's not right.

BUDDY: Well, I did. So I run away.

Pause.

PAM: Is this a joke Buddy? A sick, sick joke to upset me?

BUDDY: Real. I can still hear the blood bubbling in his throat.

PAM: Shouldn't have.

BUDDY: No.

PAM: Shouldn't have.

BUDDY: I know.

PAM: You was only in for stealing cars and now you've murdered a screw. They'll . . . they'll kill you Buddy.

BUDDY: I went to Auntie Connie's.

PAM: You should have hid there.

BUDDY: The police was there. I gave her a duck.

PAM: A what?

BUDDY: A dead duck.

PAM: I don't mind you killing ducks Buddy – but killing screws! (*Pause.*) You're contaminated. (*She pours a larger whisky.*) Like they say, there's nothing like money to attract money.

Same with us. Someone crooked in the family – and villainy is like the natural course. For you. Just 'cause Ronnie had form, they kept their eye out for you. And now you've made it worse.

BUDDY: Are you mad at me?

PAM: No, not mad love. Just helpless. And tight round me belly. Like all the air's gone out of me lungs and they're squashed together. How did you get here?

BUDDY: Nicked a motor and dumped it.

PAM: Nicked another one! Bad enough killing a screw without making it worse by nicking another car.

BUDDY: I had to.

PAM: Didn't dump it here?

BUDDY: Dumped it at Mile End. Then got the tube.

PAM: You didn't do it on purpose, did you Buddy?

BUDDY: It was an accident.

PAM: Then go back and say you're sorry and it was an accident –

BUDDY: Pam, don't be stupid.

Pause.

PAM: Ronnie'll know what to do for the best.

BUDDY: Pam, please don't keep getting drunk.

PAM: Ronnie's in Walnut Close now. The posh houses in the big gardens. He's burgling them.

BUDDY: What house?

PAM: The bloke from the airport wrote it down.

BUDDY: Airport?

PAM: Heathrow. He gets the addresses from the flight reservations and gives them to Ronnie. Ronnie is smart. His brilliance – if he weren't bent he could be Prime Minister. (*Finds list.*) 14 Walnut Close . . . or is it 17?

BUDDY: I'll go there then.

PAM: Yeah. (*Pours another drink.*) Don't get drunk you say. In this family?

BUDDY: Ronnie will help me, won't he? Got another fag?

PAM: Take the packet.

BUDDY: Better than the prison baccy.

He takes the cigarettes, kisses her briefly on the forehead and exits. PAM *stands and addresses the audience as back projection shows beautiful, rich houses, dwelling on the Christmas decorations in their illuminated windows. Spotlight on* PAM.

PAM: Baccy and chocolate. That's all they think about inside. When Ronnie goes down again, I'll leave him. I've had enough. No house in Teneriffe, not really. And I'll get a man who ain't got a record so that we can adopt a baby. They wouldn't let us adopt because of Ronnie's record. I ain't got a record! But see it's catching. Life of Riley for him. Nursery full of colour teles and hiding the stolen jewellery in the kiddies' sandpit down there in the yard. Full privileges on remand. When Ronnie came out last time, he was all suntanned. And I'd lost a stone working in the laundry. Baccy and chocolate, that's all they think about inside. And how they'll slice up their wives if they so much as let another bloke grope them. Let alone, you know. Life of Riley for Ronnie, but not Buddy, no not Buddy if they find him. They will find him. They'd found him before he'd even done anything. He was already contaminated, because of Ronnie. Know what I mean? 14 Walnut Close must be such a nice house. Or is it 17? Funny writing . . .

Light fades on PAM *and police radio messages about search for* BUDDY *as lights go up on* JOAN *sitting on a stool writing Christmas cards and talking on a wall telephone. A massive deep freeze behind her and Christmas decorations. Police radio fades to Satie, and Satie fades after she has begun speaking. She is in her early thirties, very Christian Dior.*

JOAN: Yes, Satie. I often feel like playing Satie. Not that I can play Satie.

Being unable to play the piano is a severe handicap. If you can play the piano you are a much sought after guest. You are always welcomed by people who have pianos. Especially by people who have pianos and yet are unable to play them. I can play Catch a Falling Star on one finger but I find that a good deal less than rewarding. I love reading magazine articles about social accomplishments. I read something fascinating in the hairdressers about being a perfect guest and a perfect host. Yes, um – how to hold a plate in one hand and glass of chilled Chablis in the other, while managing to eat a chicken's leg without getting your hands greasy. And what to do if whilst holding a plate in one hand and a glass of chilled Chablis in the other, your knicker elastic breaks and they slide down to your ankles. Apparently it happens not infrequently. What you do is, you calmly step out of them and place them in your handbag while saying something so rivetting and extraordinarily fascinating that nobody notices. I spent days selecting an extraordinary thing to say in the event of such an emergency. I thought I'd say: 'Look behind the rose bushes. Isn't that the dustman fucking Princess Margaret?'

BUDDY *enters, hesitates.*

The boy from the garage is here Edna. Toodaloo. (*Replaces phone receiver.*) I didn't hear you knock.

BUDDY: Wrong house, I wanted number 14, bye.

JOAN: This is number 14. Put it in the garage, did you?

BUDDY: Eh?

JOAN: The car?

BUDDY: Car.

JOAN: My car. Surely it's ready by now. Only a fault on the clutch, Mr Jameson said, though I'm sure he'll have charged me for a new gear box.

BUDDY *hypnotised by the open deep freeze.*

BUDDY: All this food!

JOAN: I beg your pardon?

BUDDY: So much. All this, so much of it! What is this, a nosh shop?

JOAN: You are the carman, aren't you?

BUDDY (*so amazed by the house, the deep freeze*): I've never been in a house like this, see.

JOAN: O . . . (*Smiles.*) I see. Not really imposing . . .

BUDDY: But impressive. (*Hand over head.*)

JOAN: Well perhaps. Are you unwell?

BUDDY: Bit . . . sick.

PAM: There's a bug about.

BUDDY: I heard about it.

JOAN: You put my Fiesta in the garage, did you?

BUDDY: Yeah, yeah. So many nice things. Here. So much food.

JOAN: More economic. Inflation the way it is. Lambs are cheaper if you buy them whole.

BUDDY: I couldn't agree more.

JOAN: How much do I owe you?

BUDDY: Owe me?

JOAN: For the car?

BUDDY: Yeah, yeah, right. Clutch, well . . . twenty-four quid. Say twenty-five, call it quits.

JOAN: Is that all?

BUDDY: O. Yeah, see, it weren't as bad as we thought. A leak in your clutch fluid canister and it got in the cable.

JOAN: O, don't destroy me with technical arguments.

BUDDY: That's handy. I had better push off then lady. (*Anxious to go.*)

JOAN: The bill?

BUDDY: I forgot it. Dashing here to get your wheels back, like.

JOAN: Wheels?

BUDDY: What we in my trade call cars.

JOAN: Wheels. How sweet.

JOAN: Happy Christmas.

JOAN: Here's thirty. (*Hands him six five notes.*) Half the Christmas box for you, half for Mr Jameson.

BUDDY: Very decent of you.

JOAN: I haven't seen you at the garage before, have I?

BUDDY: Hidden out of the way, in case I frighten the punters, harr.

Pause. JOAN *is very charming and a little flirting to him.*

JOAN: My husband . . . O, don't forget the bill. For the dreaded VAT man. Curses!

BUDDY: Curses!

JOAN: Would you like a drink?

BUDDY: Well, look . . . I think I'd better go lady.

JOAN: Don't be shy.

BUDDY: Nar . . .

JOAN: O do have a drink. Christmas drinkies.

BUDDY: Well –

JOAN: A gin?

BUDDY: Light ale please.

JOAN: Yes, a gin it is. (*She begins to pour a very large one.*) Say *quand.*

BUDDY: Beg your pardon?

JOAN: Say 'when.'

BUDDY: About half a gallon ago. Bit light headed . . . no food for . . . .

JOAN: There. (*Hands him glass.*)

BUDDY: Cheers then. Help the flu. And me toothache.

JOAN: You've got toothache?

BUDDY: Yeah.

JOAN: O, my husband's a dentist.

BUDDY: Really? Great!

JOAN: But he's away at a conference today.

BUDDY: O . . .

JOAN: And he's still waiting for the new Jaguar. And I was thinking . . . (*Seductive.*) The waiting list at your garage. I was wondering if there was some *periferique,* as it were, around it. Mmm?

BUDDY: You what?

JOAN: Some by-pass of the waiting list, if you know what I mean.

BUDDY: You want a knocked-off Jag?

JOAN: What?

BUDDY: Sorry. Slip of the tongue.

JOAN: Mister?

BUDDY: Clark.

JOAN: No relation to the Seymour-Clarks?

BUDDY: Nar.

JOAN: Mister Clark, we understand one another. I am prepared to pay above the list price for the first offer.

BUDDY: A Jag?

JOAN: When I brought the car in this morning, I noticed that in your window there was a new model, exactly the colour my husband wants, in your showroom.

BUDDY: Oh yeah. Lovely colour.

JOAN: Lovely colour. And a sign on the window, it said: 'Sold.'

BUDDY: The waiting list, see.

JOAN: I am prepared to pay a little extra to get it.

BUDDY: Well, in this life you have to pay for what you fancy.

JOAN: I knew you'd understand.

BUDDY: How much?

JOAN: A hundred pounds?

BUDDY (*amazed*): A hundred quid?

JOAN (*thinking this inadequate*): A hundred and fifty?

BUDDY (*quietly*): A hundred and fifty . . .

JOAN: We agree?

BUDDY: All right.

JOAN: And I take delivery?

BUDDY: All that.

JOAN: Tomorrow? You see, we're going to Paris for Christmas, to stay with friends and it would be so lovely to go in the new Jaguar.

BUDDY: Why not? If you've got the bread . . . (*Looks in deep freeze.*) So many loaves in here.

JOAN (*going to him at deep freeze*): Stocked up during the last baker's strike.

BUDDY: Don't miss a trick, do you, lady?

JOAN (*hands him ten pound notes*): Here, take it. I'll ring Mister Jameson in half an hour, so no tricks.

BUDDY: How could I compete with your tricks, lady? More bread in here than . . . (*Rummages inside deep freeze.*) Here, what's this?

JOAN: Offals.

BUDDY: Eh?

JOAN: Brains. A delicacy, my husband loves them.

BUDDY: Who's? Who's brains?

JOANS: Pigs I think. Frozen. A delicacy.

BUDDY: And this? (*Lifts a frozen eel.*)

JOAN: Eels. Do you mind? Should there be any grease or oil on your hands . . . the hygiene risk . . .

BUDDY: Contaminates them, eh?

He twiddles with the frozen eel. Suddenly it is a weapon, a sword. He moves the pointed head to JOAN, *then presses it against her throat.*

BUDDY: Interesting, what I'm saying, in't it. Very interesting. What is it?

JOAN: Very interesting.

BUDDY: Yeah. Hundred and fifty quid, eh? Just like that. Just like that! The car I nicked weren't even worth a hundred and fifty quid. 1970 Cortina. Clapped out heap of junk, not even worth a hundred and fifty. Not worth what you peel out like peanuts. Know what I got for it?

Pause. JOAN *makes a dash for the telephone.* BUDDY *pulls the lead out of the wall and threatens her with the sword again.*

I said: Do you know what I got for it? Guess.

JOAN: Three hundred pounds?

BUDDY: No, more, more. Don't play innocent.

JOAN: I've no idea . . . what you're talking about. I don't know what you're doing or –

BUDDY: I nicked a motor, right? Rusting shit, not the first I admit but . . . worth, value . . . one hundred and fifty greenuns. What did I get for it?

JOAN: Five hundred pounds?

BUDDY: See me hair? They take everything. Why take your hair and all. (*Scratches his short hair.*) They gave me eighteen months, lady. They locked me up, out of the way, in a prison for eighteen months.

JOAN: So, you're not the mechanic at the garage?

BUDDY: Ain't I seen you on Mastermind?

JOAN: What do you want?

Pause.

BUDDY: Dunno, lady. You're more a villain than me. Me brother-in-law, he says, says: 'Anyone with bread like this, they ain't got it legal.' I'm a villain . . .

He sits on the deep freeze, shivers. He holds in one hand the screw's silver whistle. He dangles it on its chain, like a hypnotist.

Tooth on fire, lady. Needles in me head. On fire. (*Very slowly, now.*) I done the biggun. The biggun. (*Holds his head again.*) I done the murder. The one you used to have to swing for . . . Know what I mean? Nice here, nice. (*Jumps off the deep freeze.*) Tell me one thing? This really number 14?

JOAN: Yes . . .

BUDDY: Be glad you don't live at number 17, lady. Won't let you off with a frozen eel there tonight. (*Drops the eel, exits, blackout.*)

During the blackout, another police radio message. In the blackout, we hear voices.

RONNIE: All the lights out?

AL: Yeah. Can you hear him Ronnie?

RONNIE: He's round the back now. Coming this way. Hear him?

AL: I can fucking hear him.

RONNIE: Me heart's thumping like a piston engine.

AL: Fuck it, fuck it. Shall we make a run?

RONNIE: No, Pandas out the front. No sign of the law or nothing.

AL: Sounds like . . . definitely only one of them. Bit light footed. Might be a fucking Japanese.

RONNIE: Japanese, what you talking about? Fucking Japanese?

AL: Or a Chinaman, they're small and all.

RONNIE: He's trying the French window.

We become accustomed to the darkness. We see the frame of the French window upstage centre.

AL: O Jesus. I thought you said they was in the West Indies?

RONNIE: Behind this curtain here. Soon as his head's in, let it go.

AL: Metal bar. Like the milkman. Parted his hair.

RONNIE: No fucking mistake Al.

We see a shadowy figure trying the French windows from the outside. AL *stands one side of window with a metal bar raised.* RONNIE *stands the other side. The window opens, enter a figure. Smash as the metal bar strikes the window frame.*

AL: Missed the cunt.

Sound of BUDDY *falling, yelling.*

BUDDY: Ronnie, Ronnie – leave off, it's only me.

RONNIE: You cunt.

Lights on. AL *wears a stocking over his head. A great pile of tvs, coats, jewellery etc. beside* RONNIE *who has just switched on the light.*

RONNIE: You stupid little bleeder. You daft bastard. You've made me piss me new trousers.

BUDDY: Sorry.

RONNIE: I only fucking bought them yesterday.

AL: Who is he? (*He still stands holding the metal bar, blinking with surprise.*)

RONNIE: Pam's fucking brother. You nerk, you daft prat. What do you think you're doing?

BUDDY: I come . . . to find you . . .

RONNIE: We're working, son, working! Big night tonight. Very big night.

AL: Ronnie, you've pissed your trousers.

RONNIE: Bleeding best ones ain't they.

AL: They look like your new ones.

RONNIE: They are me new ones! Might have had a bloody heart attack. Might have had.

RONNIE *kicks in the screen of a TV set.*

Now look what you've made me done.

AL: Look what you've made Ronnie done.

RONNIE: Me bloody nerves like fuses popping all over me chest, you loon.

AL: He's a bloody loon.

RONNIE: He is.

AL: I heard you say.

BUDDY: Ronnie . . . what do I do? (*Pause.*) Pam said, ask you – what to do.

RONNIE: What you talking about? I mean, what do you mean? Can't you see, you flat footed ponce –

AL: Oi. I've got flat feet. (*Takes the stocking off his head.*)

RONNIE: No offence, Al.

AL: If I hadn't got flat feet, I'd have

been a copper.

RONNIE: I'm talking about him.

AL: Bloody flat footed ponce.

RONNIE: A lot of organising has gone into this night, Buddy. A lot of very detailed planning involving a lot of very talented people and you have just strolled in right nonchalant and stuffed a fucking candelabra up me arsehole. (*Kicks in another TV screen.*) Al, you should have splattered his skull.

BUDDY: I broke out.

RONNIE: Eh, what?

BUDDY: Broke out, over the wall, on the run. And . . . this screw got killed.

BUDDY *holds his head again. Pause.*

It was an accident.

RONNIE: Listen . . . you kidding me?

BUDDY: Accident. Really.

RONNIE: Screw dead?

AL: A screw. Bleeding bloody Buddah. Prat.

RONNIE: You knocked off a fucking screw? My God! There'll be Concordes crashing on your head, boy. That is not done, that is not right, that is too much.

AL: Bleeding bloody Buddah, you prat!

BUDDY: Please Ronnie, do something. Help me.

RONNIE: Help you? Help you? God Almighty and all his angels cannot help you, kiddo. You have done what is never done. No-one murders screws.

AL: A bloke in Parkhurst murdered a screw once.

RONNIE: I'm talking about him.

AL: Mind you, it was the first time he'd been abroad.

BUDDY: Didn't mean it. I've got toothache.

RONNIE (*heavy sarcasm*): O, he had toothache! Poor little sod. Nothing wrong with knocking off a screw if you've got toothache.

BUDDY (*clings to him*): Please Ronnie, I've been everywhere else.

RONNIE: If anyone saw you come here . . . Fucking idiot. (*Throws* BUDDY *off.*)

AL: Idiot. Come on, better split.

RONNIE: Two grand here, two grand. Two fucking Gs boy. That's what you've smashed up.

AL: I'll get the motor.

AL *exits.* RONNIE *breathes furiously and tears up a fur coat. Stands panting, kicks jewellery.*

RONNIE: Do you know what you have done? With your obscene perverted presence here? You have blown months of planning, of chatting up the geezer from Heathrow with double scotches like there's no tomorrow. You have fucked it all up! Kaboosh, kaputt. Old Bill'll be round our flat like greased fucking lightning now.

BUDDY: When I broke out, I didn't know you had a big night on.

RONNIE: Should I have sent you a telegram? First thing they'll do, right? Be round your mum's. Then round Pam's. You cunt. The flat's full of gear! I just hope Sid's picked it up by now. I'll have to dump the jewellery in the kid's sand-pit outside.

BUDDY: I didn't know!

RONNIE: Why didn't you just keep away? You're on your own. Law of decency that. Villains' code. Do not contaminate others with what you have done when what you have done is disgusting even by villains' code. Scum.

RONNIE: Ronnie, please.

AL *enters. Sound of a revving car off.*

AL: We'd better leave all this and get away. Fast.

RONNIE: Yeah, and warn Frank at Heathrow before the law starts sniffing the snot up his nostrils. (*To* BUDDY.) If I go down again because of you, you leading them onto me . . . (*Pause.*) I'll fucking slice you. And that's a promise. Comprendi?

BUDDY: Sorry.

RONNIE: You will be. (*He puts on long leather overcoat.*)

AL: Come on.

RONNIE (*to* AL): He'll be sorry.

AL: He will be sorry.

BUDDY: What shall I do?

RONNIE: Dig a grave. (*Exits.*)

AL: Yeah, dig a grave. For yourself.

RONNIE *and* AL *exit through the French windows.* BUDDY *watches them go, then takes off his raincoat and selects a fur-hooded anorak and puts that on, transferring cigarettes etc from pockets. He dwells, holding the screw's silver whistle.*
Sound of 'Silent Night' off. He freezes, then relief when he realises it's carol singers. They knock on front door, still singing. BUDDY *exits through the French windows, switching off the light.*
The carol continues in the blackout, then lights up on a hospital bed. A blood drip.
A PRIEST *in vestments stands at the foot of the bed. The carol continues. There are three candles lit on the bed table.*

PRIEST: God the father of mercies/ Through the death and resurrection of His Son/Has reconciled the world to himself/And sent the Holy Spirit among us/For the forgiveness of sins;/ Through the Ministry of the Church/ May God give your pardon and peace/ And I absolve you from your sins/In the name of the Father and of the Son and of the Holy Spirit, Amen.

BUDDY *has entered holding a candle.*

BUDDY: Amen.

The PRIEST *looks at* BUDDY. BUDDY *sets the candle on the table.*

BUDDY: Hello. How is she?

PRIEST: Are you a relative?

BUDDY: She's me mum.

PRIEST: Your mother?

BUDDY: I'm her son.

PRIEST: You're Buddy?

BUDDY: Yeah. She don't arf look ill.

PRIEST: She's had a considerable transfusion. You always look like that after a transfusion.

BUDDY: Me sister, she don't reckon she's at all well. Do you come to everyone here?

PRIEST: Yes, I do.

BUDDY: You don't just come to people who are . . . you know.

PRIEST: No. She is . . . very poorly.

BUDDY: Your choir? Sounds nice. None of them in football boots.

PRIEST: The choir?

BUDDY: At me sister's wedding, noticed the choir, when they pushed off at the end, under their dresses –

PRIEST: Cassocks.

BUDDY: Yeah. They was wearing football boots. Dashing off to a match.

PRIEST: Your mother, Buddy –

BUDDY: She don't look at all well.

PRIEST: She told me you were in Borstal.

Pause.

BUDDY: I was.

PRIEST: You've finished there?

BUDDY: Ah. Look, what are you doing now?

PRIEST: Going home for my tea.

BUDDY: I wonder if I could have a word with you?

PRIEST: By all means.

Pause.

You say, you've just left Borstal? When did you leave?

BUDDY: Not long ago.

PRIEST: What do you want to tell me?

BUDDY: Um, see . . . people will think I've committed a sin.

PRIEST: Yes?

BUDDY: When I say I've left Borstal

. . . the thing is, they don't know I've left.

PRIEST: I see.

BUDDY: I thought perhaps you could go and have a word with them. Like, when you get a bit panicky – see, I got a bit panicky – when you're panicky, you don't know what to do.

PRIEST: Am I to understand that you've absconded . . . I mean, run away?

BUDDY: Absconded, yeah.

PRIEST: Why did you? Your mother was very happy that you were going to be released after Christmas.

BUDDY: She don't look too happy now, does she? You see . . . there was this accident and I got worried.

PRIEST: What sort of accident? To make you leave?

BUDDY: O Christ! Sorry . . . you see . . . ah . . . um . . .

PRIEST: Take your time, explain in your own words. You had an accident?

BUDDY: I didn't. He did. Did you see the film *Soldier Blue*?

PRIEST: No.

BUDDY: Pity. See, they was playing football and when the ball went over the wall, I had to get it and it was on the river, on the ice, and I found this dead duck and I got this plank to get the ball because I couldn't reach and this Henderson –

PRIEST: Another boy?

BUDDY: Nar, a screw –

PRIEST: A warder?

BUDDY: Yeah, he come out to see what I was doing and we had this chat about this duck because he likes ducks – well, he used to and . . . there was this accident.

Pause.

PRIEST: Is that all?

BUDDY: I've got toothache. And he was nice to me. He was going to get a dentist and I was getting the plank and I turned round and hit him with the plank and, this is ridiculous (*Giggles.*). It's funny. But it ain't 'cause, the plank hit him and the spike went in him and . . . I thought he was joking. And . . .

Pause.

BUDDY: He was dead. And I run. I've been all over the place and I reckoned you could have a word with them and explain it was an accident.

PRIEST: Was it an accident?

BUDDY: 'Course it was an accident.

PRIEST: You didn't mean to kill him?

BUDDY: I didn't kill him! He just died. I swear, I swear on me mum's life . . . I know they won't believe it. Do you believe it?

PRIEST: I want to know . . . more about it.

BUDDY: It sounds stupid.

PRIEST: It sounds a little unlikely.

BUDDY: Yeah.

PRIEST: Do you have a record of violence?

BUDDY: TDA . . . Taking and driving away . . . nicking cars, that's all. She looks terrible.

PRIEST: She's –

BUDDY: They'll murder me.

PRIEST: Why do you think the authorities will disbelieve you?

BUDDY: They don't trust no-one.

PRIEST: But surely that's part of their jobs, as policemen.

BUDDY: Look, do you believe me? That it was an accident?

PRIEST: Yes, I do.

BUDDY (*amazed*): Why?

PRIEST: I believe you because, the utter idiocy of it all. That, I think, is in your favour. (*Looks at his watch.*)

BUDDY: You in a hurry?

PRIEST: No.

BUDDY: Good, 'cause what I want you

to do for me – you will do it for me, won't you? – what I'd like you to do is, go there to the Borstal and . . . tell them it was an accident. For me.

PRIEST: Wouldn't it be better if you came with me to corroborate what you want me to say?

BUDDY: They'll think, if I'm there, they won't believe me.

PRIEST: Assuming it was, as you say, an accident . . . are you firm in your decision not to go back?

BUDDY: I'd explain to them, but they won't listen.

PRIEST: It'll be difficult for me to persuade them, to convince them that it was an accident.

BUDDY: You've got a better chance than I have.

PRIEST: So, if I go to the governor and explain, plead your case, your side . . . where will you stay? Your mother's flat? (*Pause.*) Shall I find a place for you to stay?

BUDDY: Do you mean that?

PRIEST: I do. But you will have to go back there eventually. You're afraid of the consequences of being charged with a murder?

BUDDY: Don't say that!!!

PRIEST: A killing. I can't promise you any results. You must trust me.

BUDDY: How can I trust that you believe me?

PRIEST: It's bizarre enough to be the truth. I shall tell them that it was an accident and do my best to ensure that the authorities are unbiased when . . . you face them.

BUDDY: You'll go now then?

PRIEST: Let us pause a moment and . . . quietly pray.

Pause. The PRIEST *stands in silent prayer.* BUDDY *takes the money* JOAN *had given him from his pocket and puts in on the bed near the* PRIEST. *He is nervous at the inactivity. Suddenly the bell sounds.* BUDDY *panics and dashes off. The* PRIEST *calls after him:*

PRIEST: Buddy, Buddy – that was only the bell for the end of visiting. Buddy.

The PRIEST *begins to run after him as Blackout. Music loud: latest top single hit, very loud. Then flashing coloured lights of an amusement arcade and* BUDDY *wheels on a one-armed bandit to stage centre. He speaks directly to the audience as pop songs continue quietly in the background:*

BUDDY: Fuck me, dishing out the vicar a hundred and fifty quid and me without a penny in me pocket. (*Takes a beer can tag from his pocket and spits on it.*) These Southend blokes in there, they told me how to do it. They made a fortune on the bandits with a beer can tag and the juice. What you need is a little squirt of the old three in one motor oil. Three in one motor oil, like you use in the carbs, know what I mean? Jams the machine. Fucks the mechanism. Trade secret, I'm telling you. (*Laughs.*) Put the tag in . . . (*Puts the tag in the coin slot. Bangs the machine, shakes it.*) Count ten, give the oil time to ooze the motor . . . one, two, three, four, five, six, seven, eight, nine, ten and . . . Jackpot!

Hundreds of coins pour out. BUDDY *kneels to collect them. Enter* DAVE, *same age, with crash helmet.*

DAVE: Oi . . .

BUDDY (*leaps up, shocked*): Fucking hell . . .

DAVE (*very nervous*): Christ, are you up to here in it.

BUDDY: Thanks for coming Dave.

DAVE: You shouldn't have phoned me. Shouldn't have.

BUDDY: You give me your number.

DAVE: For when you was out legit. Not . . . I'm straight now, straight, ain't I? Don't want to go back there.

BUDDY: Thanks for coming.

DAVE: Here.

BUDDY: You got it?

DAVE: Me sister got it, from the chemists.

BUDDY: I remember you said she works in a chemists. Tar.

DAVE: It's an emergency filling. It's kinda like chewing gum, see. Heat it up in hot water and then stick it in your tooth and . . . Christ. The size of your face.

BUDDY (*pockets the emergency filling*): Thanks Dave.

DAVE: I shouldn't be here. If the law found me here with you . . . Christ. Which one was it?

BUDDY: Henderson.

DAVE: The Donald Duck bloke?

BUDDY: Yeah. (*Behaves a little nonchalantly because of* DAVE's *awe.*)

DAVE: He was a nice bloke, not like the others. Why him?

BUDDY: It was an accident.

DAVE: In the chest. Jesus Buddy – ain't like you.

BUDDY: I was standing outside to get the ball and . . . match with the village team –

DAVE: Who won?

BUDDY: We was winning three-one. Jamie scored two.

DAVE: Jamie's a cart-horse. Always beat the village poufs. Nicking the machines . . . it works then: What the Southend blokes said.

BUDDY *pockets the remainder of the coins.*

BUDDY: They all got a year. Woman tonight, posh woman – she gave me a hundred and fifty quid to jump the queue for her for a new Jag.

DAVE: You're joking!

BUDDY: A hundred and fifty quid in tenners. What I nicked weren't worth that.

DAVE: Well, that's not the point, is it?

BUDDY: Why ain't it? (*Pause.*) Why ain't it?

DAVE (*laughs unsurely*): You and your questions! Giggles with the trick cyclist. Why why why . . .

BUDDY: He couldn't answer them. Can you?

DAVE: For fuck's sake, Buddy. I went out on a limb to bring the thing for your tooth. I'm going.

BUDDY (*shouts, pleads*): Someone's gotta help me!

DAVE: Your mum –

BUDDY: She's in hospital again –

DAVE: Sorry. (*Jittery.*) Look, I've gotta go now. Say the Old Bill clock me here, accomplice or something . . .

BUDDY: Why did they keep picking on me?

DAVE: They're fucking entitled to now, after what you've done.

BUDDY: What?

DAVE: Murdering a screw.

Pause. It sinks in. Just the pop song and the flashing coloured lights.

BUDDY: Say that again.

DAVE: Eh?

BUDDY: Say me name and then . . . say what I've done.

DAVE: How do you mean?

BUDDY: I . . . I . . . (*Pause.*) I can't believe it, see.

DAVE: Buddy . . .

BUDDY: Yeah?

DAVE: Buddy, on the news on the telly . . . I was having me tea . . . there was this photo of you and they said, Kenneth Kendall said: police wished to interview you to help them with their inquiries following the murder of a screw at the Borstal. You, they said. There was this photo, of you.

Pause.

BUDDY: I'm only 17.

DAVE: They never said that. You had long hair in the photo.

BUDDY: They take everything. Why

take your hair and all? They'll find me soon.

DAVE: They always do. Look, what you want to do is . . .

Pause.

BUDDY: What?

DAVE: Go somewhere, to someone, like . . . who you can trust. Who'll hide you and protect you so they won't rough you up. Someone who'll . . .

Pause.

BUDDY: Like who?

DAVE: There must be *someone.*

BUDDY: Yeah there must be. Ain't Ronnie, though. Ain't Pam, ain't me mum, ain't the priest, ain't Auntie Connie and ain't Uncle Harold. He's dead. And ain't the posh woman – what she does, more wrong than what I done.

DAVE: I am going now.

BUDDY: All right. Tar Dave.

DAVE: How did the spuds I planted come up?

BUDDY: Really nice. Dug 'em up for Christmas dinner. Dave . . .

DAVE: What?

BUDDY: Did it ever seem to you, like . . . when you was in there . . . you know some of them . . . their faces, their eyes . . . you knew they was going to be in there, or another prison, always be there, all their lives . . . Did it seem like that to you? Like, it'd be the place you was always gonna be?

Pause.

DAVE: Better be going. So cold, looks like it'll snow tonight.

BUDDY: Can I come and stay the night at your flat?

DAVE: For Christ's sake Buddy. Don't ask me that. 'Course you can't. I'm a reformed person now. Gonna get a job.

BUDDY: Ain't you had one?

DAVE: Not since I was released. There's a helluva shortage. But then, I ain't got into no more trouble neither.

BUDDY: Thank your sister for me.

DAVE *nods and goes.*
Cut music. Blackout, but:
Spotlight on BUDDY *fingering the whistle.*

BUDDY (*to the audience*): There was this madman in the park. Years ago, scared away the kids. Ran past him. He only had one leg. The othr one was wooden. Then one winter, it snowed a lot . . .

Snowflakes begin to fall. Dim lights on empty stage. The back projection is of a deserted dockside at night.

And the madman disappeared. And when the weather warmed up and the snow melted they found his body in the pond in the park. And when all the snow had gone, they found his wooden leg and on it he had carved: 'Goodbye cruel world.'

Voice off singing First World War song 'Good-byee'.
A tractor tyre on a rope is lowered – an impromptu swing. BUDDY *swings on it. There is a snow covered sand-pit stage centre.*

The singing gets nearer.

VOICE: Shut up.

VOICE 2: The kids in here are trying to get to sleep.

VOICE 3: I'll come down there and lay you out, you dirty, smelling, child-molesting cunt.

Enter SAMMY, *in tramp clothes – old army uniform. He finishes the song.* BUDDY *laughs. Snow falls more heavily.*

SAMMY: Snowing.

BUDDY: Yeah.

SAMMY: Can you lend me a bob or two.

BUDDY: Help yourself.

BUDDY *tosses a handful of bandit coins onto the snow of the kid's sand-pit.*

SAMMY: Thank you, thank you. But it would have been a hell of a lot easier if you'd . . .

He gets on his knees to pick them up.

There's sand underneath here.

BUDDY: Sand-pit for the kids in the flats.

SAMMY: So high, all around. So many towers. You live here?

BUDDY: Sort of. On and off.

SAMMY: I have not a home myself.

BUDDY: I figured that.

SAMMY: I move around. Have to get pissed tonight, I will. Then I'll be warm.

BUDDY: How's that?

SAMMY: Find me in the gutter, lock me up. The police will. Bed and breakfast. That's home. When it's too cold to be out on the streets. Ice at night.

BUDDY: Yeah.

SAMMY: Your face is swollen – been fighting?

BUDDY: Nar.

SAMMY: I was a fighter. Fighting – it's the highest and honourablest action for any man. You must fight boy. Eyes full of fear. Searching eyes. You in trouble boy?

BUDDY: You could say that.

SAMMY *beats his hands with cold, puts them under his armpits.*

SAMMY: Never as bad as it seems. Never.

BUDDY *laughs, swings higher.*

Don't laugh at me, don't laugh at me, boy. Old tramp, that right? Old nothing in his ragged clothes, shit under his finger-nails. Fighter boy, me. Fighter. I could biff. I could wallop. Don't be frightened of me. See your eyes. See, you know. Prison face. Whatever you've done – Old eyes in a child's face. No innocence there. What you done, boy?

BUDDY *swings, turning his back on* SAMMY. *Snow is falling still more heavily.*

When I'm pissed they give me bread and breakfast at the nick. Blood and snot, that was me. I was a boxer, boy. Sammy the name.

He drinks from a beer bottle, then hands it to BUDDY.

Me father, he was a boxer too. Died in the Barking Canal. Got pissed, fell in then come to the surface three times and drowned. He was waiting for the count of eight. (*Laughs.*) I had four fights a week. When the weather was good, followed the summer fairs. When winter come, the cities. Booths in the fairgrounds at the end, with the freak shows. Some nights, as the snow fell, hands so numb with the cold I could hardly make a fist. I got me title. One night, I got me title. The finest fighter in the land. Piss me trousers now. Shamed meself last time I was in the dock of the court. I shitted. Lost control of me bowels, see. Coppers had to mop it up. Sneered at me, laughed at me, turned up their noses. 'All right,' I says. 'Who do you think you're snotting at? Do what you like to me, take away from me what you like. One thing you can never do. You can never take away the night I won me title.' Whatever becomes of me, they can never take away the night I won me title.

BUDDY: Whatever becomes of me . . . never take away the night I spiked a screw.

Pause. BUDDY *stops swinging.*

SAMMY: There's a man who helps boys in trouble. Albert. Albert his name, they call him Lord Plaistow now. I been to him. I've had troubles. Trust him. Fine man. Times no-one'll help, Albert, Lord Plaistow, he'll help. Tell you where he lives, give you his phone number. Always phone him up, in trouble. Here.

Hands BUDDY *a paper from his tobacco tin.*

Say Sammy sent you, Sammy who one night was British lightweight champion.

BUDDY *gets off the swing, pockets*

the address.

SAMMY: You'll need money for the phone, money for the fare.

SAMMY *hands* BUDDY *some coins.* BUDDY *nods, then exits.*

SAMMY: Never take away the night I won . . . Never take away the day he . . .

Kneels and buries his hands in the sand-pit.

Good God! There's necklaces in the sand.

Holds up necklaces and rings.

And watches and rings and jewellery and . . . God thank you. For such a reward for one little act of kindness.

He laughs.
Blackout.
Music: John Lennon's 'So This Is Christmas' from the album Shaved Fish.

End of Act One

ACT TWO

Music before act: Lennon's 'So This Is Christmas'.
Lights up on an elegant room full of Christmas decorations; a tree, presents etc. The table is laid for a dinner party. EDNA, *about 50, and dressed very elegantly, enters, and addresses the audience as the music fades. She wears a brightly-coloured paper Christmas party hat.*

EDNA: Guests will be arriving by the minute. A dinner party to celebrate the Christmas recess. Henry's cooking. He loves to cook. And I must switch on the fairy lights.

She switches on twinkling tree lights.

Fairy lights create such a warm ambience. And hide my wrinkles. They are especially plentiful around my neck, which is why I wear so many pearls. And music! Guitar concerto.

Guitar concerto on hi-fi. Rodrigues.

Love this. Reminds me of our holidays in Spain. Granada, Marbella, Lorett, Salami.

HENRY'S VOICE: No salami tonight Edna. Ha ha.

EDNA (*sits elegantly*): Need a hand darling?

HENRY'S VOICE: No thanks, Edna. Wait till you taste this paté. Yum yum.

EDNA: Henry is so tired since he's been a Minister. A junior minister. He works so hard with the awful business of government and his directorships. We don't fuck much now, except on the occasional fact-finding tours. When we were young we fucked a lot. At Oxford Henry was at the university and I lived in a village outside. I lived for ponies until Henry swept me off my feet as though on some invisible great white charger. Daddy was fearfully upset when he heard Henry was a Socialist. But as I said to mummy, he *had* to be Labour or he might never have got a seat.

Enter HENRY *in a Pears Soap advert apron and with a plate of paté. He too wears a party hat. He has an occasional stutter.*

HENRY: Paté! Ex . . . ex . . . ex . . .

EDNA: Excellent? Extraordinary?

HENRY: Exquisite. Sucking pig. A real sucking pig would have been too ostentatious but paté – sucking pig.

He exits having deposited the pate on the table.

EDNA: I refuse to perform fellatio. I'm on a low calorie diet and I'm concerned at the calorie intake of the . . . thingy. Besides, the home and the children are my life. Fiona and Sarah are sweet, but I'm awfully worried at the set Adam has got himself into. At Harrow. I was alarmed when he came to the golf club wearing a safety pin in his nose. Henry wants him to read Greats at Oxford, but it's most distressing, this punk thing. I mean, when he was here at Easter, things kept appearing in his bedroom and the harness for Fiona's pony disappeared. He's gone to see the Boomtown Rats at the Rainbow tonight.

HENRY (*entering with a glass*): He jolly well ought to get his head down and get on with his w . . . w . . . work.

EDNA: Exactly.

HENRY: Garlic. (*Shows a bottle of pickled garlics, sniffs them.*)

EDNA: Henry, really! I insist.

HENRY: It is essential to the dish I am preparing.

EDNA: We cannot inflict garlic on our guests.

HENRY: Edna, you and I have had this f . . . f . . . friction before –

EDNA: I'd have preferred something more traditional anyway. A roast.

HENRY: The garlic is essential. In the Evening Standard, Delia Smith says pickle it, thereby ensuring that the qualities of the garlic that in you arouse such h . . . h . . . hostility are reduced by the process of pickling. It isn't like garlic.

EDNA: Then what is the point of having it?

HENRY: Because it is correct. For centuries the French have used the garlic in this dish to bring out the flavour and I really object to . . . Look. It's a perfect compapomise. Garlic that doesn't taste like garlic.

EDNA: I wish you'd take as much trouble with the Brussel sprouts.

HENRY: I am. (*Smells.*) Ah, tomatoes provencal. Wonderful tip old Delia – growing them in the drain.

EDNA: Please be sure not to say anything like that to Joan, not tonight. Poor Joan.

HENRY: She's been up there an awful long time.

EDNA: And Peter still not back from the conference.

HENRY: I just hope Albert behaves himself.

EDNA: You could have ensured his punctual presence by escorting him back from the bar.

HENRY: He wasn't there. He was doing his Santa Claus thingy, at Great Ormond Street.*

Cooker bell pings off.

Ah, time to heat the Espagnol sauce. (*Exits.*)

EDNA (*loud*): I saw the temperatures of the West Indies in *The Times*. I think this will be the most enjoyable winter holiday –

HENRY'S VOICE (*off*): Business trip. Work, darling, work. We really must get some renegotiations under way for their poor sugar industry. That EEC deal was appalling.

JOAN *enters, beautifully dressed, but melancholic.*

EDNA: Darling! Feeling better now?

JOAN: I just can't get over the shock.

EDNA: Of course. It must have been a frightful shock.

JOAN: It was absolutely appalling. To have been held up at knife point –

*Children's Hospital

HENRY *enters with a glass and a port bottle.*

HENRY: More, I thought, eel tail.

EDNA: Be quiet Henry

JOAN: I suppose I was lucky, being in, I mean. Two other houses in the road were ransacked. Everything stolen, the police said. And the wilful destruction of property. And the poor Woods, those clocks. They . . . they just excreted in their bed.

HENRY: I expect it was the shock at discovering the break-in.

EDNA: Henry!

JOAN: I meant, the burglars.

HENRY: Ah. Need the port for the old . . . (*Exits with the port bottle.*)

The telephone rings as JOAN *sits.*

EDNA: That'll be Albert I expect. I'm glad Lord Plaistow is coming – livens us all up.

JOAN: He always makes me laugh, he's so amusing.

EDNA: Henry says he hasn't quite been himself since they put him in the Lords. Making Albert a Lord, the thought of it! (*Speaking on the phone.*) Albert darling. What? O no. But I mean, it's Christmas! Well, can't you see him quickly and come? O do. Joan and Peter'll be here and . . . you really can't let us down. Please. (*Replaces the receiver.*) Henry. Albert on the phone. He said he might not be able to come.

Enter HENRY.

HENRY: What?

EDNA: He's had a panic phone call from some youngster from his old constituency . . . So he's staying at home to see him.

HENRY: That's q . . . q . . . quintessential Albert.

EDNA: At Christmas though?

HENRY: I do admire Albert in a way. All his stuff with kids. I'm pretty sure the emotional involvement is a mistake but –

EDNA (*sudden inspiration*): Why don't we . . .

HENRY: What?

EDNA: Why don't we ask Albert to bring the youngster here? Albert and his waifs and strays, he's always helping people in trouble, especially kids. Like his Santa Claus thingy this afternoon. He does so much that's good but never reaches the papers.

HENRY: By all accounts Crossman was asleep half the time.

EDNA: Let's ask him to bring the youngster here. I insist Henry. Lots of our friends take orphans in at Christmas. From Barnados and what have you. All I'm asking is, we ask Albert to bring the little stranger here os that we can give him a jolly decent Christmas and a nice meal.

HENRY: Edna, for goodness sake, the one thing that can be said for the Welfare State for its loopholes and shortcomings is that not many go short of a decent meal at Christmas.

EDNA: O Henry, do say yes. We have so much to share. Far more than we actually need. And it would be lovely – a real old fashioned family Christmas. It isn't really the same in the West Indies. This is our only chance tonight before we go. To share a family Christmas with a deprived youngster. I could get some of Adam's toys out of the attic and wrap them up as presents and . . . it'll be just like Christmas was when our children were young. Do agree.

HENRY: Joan, tell her she's being ridiculous.

JOAN: I'm not sure that she is. I know what she means about wanting to share. To share our good fortune with someone less fortunate than ourselves. We seriously thought about a child from one of the council homes. We might have done it if we hadn't been going to France.

HENRY: Look Edna, what do you suppose might be the effect on the child afterwards – after being subjected to a bellyful of liberal, middle-class do-gooding?

EDNA: You're so cynical. You weren't like this when I married you. You were terribly Socialist.

HENRY: I've been a professional Socialist for 20 years now Edna and –

JOAN: I don't think of you as a Socialist Henry. You're a Minister.

HENRY: Look, I want to make my position on this absolutely clear.

EDNA: Whenever you say that, it's a euphemism for you haven't an idea in your head.

HENRY: Quite the contrary actually. The producer of *Any Questions* congratulated me on the breadth of subjects upon which I did have opinions. I was the only member of the panel who spoke as long about nappy rash as the prospect of a lasting peace formula in the Middle East.

EDNA: That's because you stutter every time you say an Arab name.

HENRY: S . . . S . . . S . . .

EDNA: Sadat?

HENRY: Sod off. (*Exits.*)

EDNA: You do think it's a good idea, don't you Joan?

JOAN: Yes.

EDNA: I shall phone Albert. The good Lord Plaistow . . .

Lights off EDNA's *room. Telephone ringing. Lights up on sofa of* LORD PLAISTOW's *room. He enters with a bottle and glass singing; he wears a Santa Claus costume. There is a sack of presents beside the sofa.*

ALBERT: When I'm leaning on the lamppost at the corner of the street
Waiting for a certain laddie to pass by,
O me, O my,
Waiting for a laddie to pass by.

Answers phone. He is a little drunk.

Hello, Lord Plaistow speaking. Edna who? Madam, I assure you I have never heard of anyone called Edna. Ah . . . of course it was a joke, Edna, dear dear Edna. Just a bit of the festive Yuletide bonhomie. O wonderful, wonderful. Seemed to have cheered the kiddies up this afternoon. I find I only have to mention Harold's last Honours List and even children laugh. Bloody disc-jockey they had there got all the attention. No-one had ever heard of me. What, the waif and stray coming here? Jolly decent of you Edna, jolly decent of you. Old friend told him to phone me so I feel a certain sense of . . . duty would be the wrong word, but I'm damned if I can think of the right one.

Doorbell rings off.

Ah, that must be my little stranger. OK Edna, we shall see, we shall see. I'll be along in half an hour anyway. We'll see about this kiddie.

Replaces telephone. On intercom:

Fine lad, fine. Door opening now. Be sure to give it a bit of a bang from behind. I'm second on the left past the lift.

Replaces intercom receiver, continues to sing and dance as he pours drink and sits. BUDDY *enters, shivering.* ALBERT *stops singing.*

ALBERT: George Formby.

BUDDY: Lord Plaistow?

ALBERT: Yes. George Formby's dead.

BUDDY: I didn't know that.

ALBERT: Did you know Marc Bolan's dead?

BUDDY: Eh?

ALBERT: I never knew he was alive.

BUDDY: He was a singer. T Rex group.

ALBERT: Little girlie at Great Ormond Street this afternoon – fearfully upset the DJ didn't have a Marc Bolan record. All these singers dropping off: Callas, Bing, Elvis. If I'd known about Bolan as well I'd have probably stopped singing in me bath. Irresistible temptation for fate.

BUDDY: Me mum liked Buddy Holly – that's why she called me Buddy.

ALBERT: Singer eh? Good job she wasn't wild about the Great Carouso. Never mind, never mind. You're shivering?

BUDDY: Getting colder. Really icy out.

ALBERT: Warm yourself in front of the fire here.

BUDDY: Real brass monkey.*

ALBERT: Can't be that bad or they would have cancelled the match tonight. Hammers are still playing.

BUDDY: O.

ALBERT: Sit down lad, a sit down. Make yourself at home. Drink? (*Pours a large whisky and gives it to* BUDDY.) So old Sammy told you to seek me out.

BUDDY: The old boxer.

ALBERT: How do you know him?

BUDDY: I met him.

ALBERT: One night he was champion of the British Isles. Hands up, arms outstretched beneath the arc lights with a golden belt clipped around his waist. Two years later – in the gutter. Couple of fights after his championship, he killed a man in the ring. O, his opponent shouldn't have been there in the first place, some head injury. But the laws were more lax then, the medical examinations less thorough. But old Sammy was prohibited from ever putting on professional gloves again – not that he ever wanted to. The death wreaked havoc on Sammy's life. I like Sammy. Spent more nights in the nick than out. I only see him when he's in trouble. About time I heard from him again. (*Pause.*) Why did you want to see me? Don't shake. You're safe here. (*Pours another drink.*) Where do you come from?

BUDDY: Plaistow.

ALBERT: Whereabouts?

BUDDY: Do you know the Greengate pub?

ALBERT: I've pissed a fortune down the Greengate's porcelain.

*Slang for freezing.

BUDDY: Well down that road – near the docks.

ALBERT: Docks closed now.

BUDDY: Yeah.

ALBERT: Have another. (*Drinks.*)

BUDDY: Tar. Making me head spin.

ALBERT: Good. Biggest docks in the world, my day – the London docks. Seen as many as 85 vessels in the Royals. Queuing up to get in – all the way from Gallion's Reach to Tower Bridge. Passed there the other week. Three vessels I counted. Three.

BUDDY: In our road, all the men worked there. Dockies.

ALBERT: Something special about a dockie. In the city, a man of the sea. Hard job.

BUDDY: Tough blokes.

ALBERT: No dockies in Plaistow now.

BUDDY: No docks.

ALBERT: On the run, are you?

Pause.

You can tell me . . .

BUDDY: I did know a bloke once. Who was on the run. From Borstal.

ALBERT: Borstal eh? I know about those places. According to the Jay report more than 11,000 out of the 12,000 kids in Borstals shouldn't be there.

BUDDY: Comedian, is he?

ALBERT: His father-in-law is. This Jay bloke is married to the Prime Minister's daughter.

BUDDY: Make them sound like the Marx brothers.

ALBERT: Listen Chubby chops, whatever you've done – it can't be that bad.

BUDDY: Nar?

ALBERT: We all make mistakes.

BUDDY: Have you?

ALBERT: I beg your pardon?

BUDDY: Lord Plaistow.

ALBERT: Yerrs.

BUDDY: Mistakes? You made?

ALBERT: Fill a Hansard.

BUDDY: A what?

ALBERT: Where they report it all, every word you say in Parliament.

BUDDY: Lord Plaistow. All grand this. All lush and smelling posh and rich things and – you called Lord Plaistow. You don't live in Plaistow. In the slums. Do you, Lord.

ALBERT: I did, once.

BUDDY: Very honoured, you know. Very honoured you call yourself Lord Plaistow.

ALBERT: A tribute to my ex-constituents, when they moved me into the Upper House.

BUDDY: Felt all honoured and flattered we did, down in the slums. I . . . I . . . (*Holds his face.*) Pain is going right into me head.

ALBERT: Your face . . . ?

BUDDY: I got some stuff, for me tooth. Got any hot water, governor?

ALBERT: Water? I suppose there must be some here somewhere . . . (*Exits.*)

BUDDY: Tooth on fire. Tooth is. Screaming in me head. Get this fixed and . . . everything'll be all right.

ALBERT *returns with a bowl.*

Won' it?

ALBERT: Poor kid . . . here, let me see.

BUDDY (*his face close to* ALBERT's): When you open your mouth, all I smell is brandy and see gold.

ALBERT: Still me own teeth.

BUDDY: Polish them with Brasso?

BUDDY *fixes the temporary filling in his mouth.* ALBERT *smiles and strokes* BUDDY's *hair.*

ALBERT: Skin so smooth. Shiny hair. And freckles around your nose. Not an ounce of spare flesh on you. (*Pause.*) You remind me about everything that was good about being young. Wide open eyes, no longer innocent. Where did you lose that, beautiful Cockney boy? With your red lips and your pale skin . . .

BUDDY: You bent? Are you?

ALBERT *pauses, then roars with laughter and tops up their two glasses.* BUDDY *sets down the bowl and puts his feet up on the sofa, hands behind his head.*

ALBERT: For God's sake, relax, boy, relax. It's . . . err . . . it's . . . oh yes, it's Christmas. Time for joy. Time for celebration. For festivity. Bit of . . . awash with happiness.

BUDDY: Happiness? After what I done?

ALBERT: Shall I get you drunk, Chubby Chops?

BUDDY: Why should I care? Safe here. Warm and safe.

ALBERT: Drink from the goblet. Drink it all down fast. Anaesthetise the pain of your tooth and your cares. Ah, dentist! Dentist! The dinner party tonight – there'll be a dentist. Chubby, I shall take you to dinner. A feast.

BUDDY: Right what I fancy.

ALBERT: But there'll be a dentist there. Woman, bit snobby, like she's got a champagne bottle permanently lodged up her arsehole – her husband's a dentist, he'll be there. We shall be on our way. If I can get a Minicab. This clobber, can't stand in the street hailing a cab. (*Laughs at* BUDDY *and winks.*) They might think I'm a pouf.

ALBERT *dials on the phone and waits.* BUDDY *bounces up and down on the sofa, laughing.*

BUDDY: I ain't stupid.

ALBERT: Nar, you ain't.

BUDDY: All your friends be there, eh?

ALBERT: Well, sort of. One does not have such a large spectrum of choice when one has . . . impaled the sanctity of one's party's image.

BUDDY: Labour Party?

ALBERT: Nothing else.

BUDDY: You don't know nothing about me.

ALBERT: Sammy sent you. That's a recommendation.

BUDDY: Are you taking the piss out of me?

ALBERT: No.

BUDDY: I'm pissed.

ALBERT: I'm pissed.

BUDDY: Where are we going then?

ALBERT: A splendid dinner. Lose your terrors tonight.

BUDDY: Are you pissing me about?

ALBERT: No. (*Pause.*) I want to kiss you . . .

BUDDY *raises his arm and fist as though to strike* ALBERT. *Then he flips his wrist in an effeminate gesture and offers the back of his hand to be kissed.* ALBERT *gropes* BUDDY's *upper thigh and laughs.*

Blackout. Football crowd roaring. Lights up on a urinal beneath the grandstand at West Ham football ground. Crowd noises continue off. RONNIE *and* AL *urinate.*

RONNIE: I feel like I've been doing this all bloody night.

AL: Handy us sneaking in the last ten minutes. They open the gates early so the poor bleeders can get out and miss the punishment, eh. (*Laughs.*)

RONNIE: What we'll do is, we'll get behind the goal. There's bound to be someone there who we know. Alibis.

AL: Still losing 1-0. By God, they're going to be relegated this season – straight into the fourth division.

They step away from urinal, zipping flies.

RONNIE: Right, this is what we'll do. Are you listening to me Al?

AL: Was that a goal?

They listen to the roar.

RONNIE: Don't know. Now knock back some of this scotch. Get a real smelly breath. What we'll do is, soon as the match finishes we'll dash down onto the pitch and knock a copper's hat off, rough him up a bit. All Christmas piss-artist's like. Perfect alibi. Cop'll arrest us. If he's arrested us for hitting him, how could we have been doing the houses in Walnut Close, eh?

AL: Brilliant Ronnie, brilliant. Your old lady, she's right. Brains like yours, you could have been Prime Minister.

RONNIE: Dumped the heavy stuff, OK. But as soon as the heat's died off, we'll dig up the jewellery from the sandpit outside the flats, right? Thousands, thousands we've stacked down there.

AL: Bastard little brother-in-law, you should have not shot him.

RONNIE: Yeah, well. All right now. Handed Pam a few sleepers so she'll be out of her head even if the Old Bill tries to give her the ol' M15.

AL: So, we was here all night?

RONNIE: From seven thirty – here at the match.

AL: Great alibi.

RONNIE: Yeah. I got this one from a geezer in the Scrubs. A little variation, mind. He didn't do the job he was in for. Swears it, the robbery. I believed him. Classy bint, bit educated like, she took him to see some fucking Italian film. All foreign. Antonioni or something. Next day the law comes round his house about this job. He says: 'No, weren't me. I went to see this film, didn't I.' They says, 'What film, what was it called?' 'Can't remember', he says. 'What was it about?' they says. 'Good fucking question,' he says. 'I don't know.' Bint had pissed off. He got eighteen months.

AL: That's why I never go to foreign films. Unless they're hard porn.

Enter SAMMY.

SAMMY: Ronnie!

RONNIE: Sammy, son. Sammy. Hello. Happy Christmas. Al here. Don't forget you saw us both here. Tonight.

SAMMY: I'm looking for someone bent.

AL: Oi, watch it!

RONNIE: Sammy listen, me and Al here – you saw us before the game started, didn't you?

SAMMY: Anything you say, Ronnie. Anything you say.

RONNIE: Good lad. (*Hands* SAMMY *a fiver.*)

SAMMY: Ronnie, that's very generous of you. But I've got something for you.

RONNIE (*laughs contemptuously*): Got to get down behind the goals, dad. Behind the goal.

SAMMY: But Ronnie, I've got some gear.

RONNIE: Knocked off nylons? (*Laughs.*)

SAMMY: Just the sort of stuff you specialise in. I got some . . . sell it to you. Looking for a fence. But, old time's sake, I'll sell it to you.

AL: Not tonight. grandad. Not tonight.

SAMMY: Always sell knocked off valuables in here – in the shit house.

RONNIE: That's a bit where we are tonight, Sammy old son. So, look piss off will you?

SAMMY: But Ronnie! Must be worth thousands and thousands. I only want a hundred or so. Necklaces and rings and watches and wonderful jewellery.

AL: Got to get down –

SAMMY: Look. (*Produces a necklace from his raincoat pocket.*) See, real class, real classy.

RONNIE *inspects it.*

RONNIE: Where did you get this?

SAMMY: Ask me no questions.

RONNIE: I am asking you, dad. Where did you get this gear?

SAMMY: A contact. I can't say.

AL: Ronnie . . . (*Looking at the necklace.*)

RONNIE (*grabbing* SAMMY's *throat*): Sammy . . . ?

SAMMY: Can't say Ronnie, can't say.

Contact, contact. Big job. Can't reveal my sources. Just offering you a bargain.

RONNIE: Can't reveal your sources? Who the bloody hell would hand you gear like this, you smelly, farting old windbag. I'll tell you where you got this gear, you child molesting old cunt. Out of the fucking sand-pit outside my flats, that's where you got it.

SAMMY: How do you know?

RONNIE: 'Cause that's where I fucking buried it, you evil, stinking old bastard.

SAMMY: It's yours?

RONNIE: Of course it's fucking mine. Al, stuff his head down the lavatory bowl, make him drown.

SAMMY: Ronnie, I'm sorry about this. I don't know what to say. Is it hot?

RONNIE: Hot he says, hot! My God, it's fucking vindaloo. Put it this way. Two hours ago, this gear here – (*Shakes* SAMMY *and discovers more jewellery in his coat.*) My God, how much more have you got here? Jesus Christ, not three hours ago this little lot was stinking of Bluebell Polish in safes all over Hornchurch.

SAMMY: I'm sorry, Ronnie. Sorry.

AL: I'll drown his head in the piss-pot.

RONNIE: Anyone see you lift it?

SAMMY: See me, see me?

RONNIE: Digging up the sandpit?

SAMMY: No, no, honest. No-one. Except a kid.

RONNIE: A kid?

SAMMY: Poor little bleeder. On the run, I think. From Borstal.

RONNIE: Jesus Christ Almighty. I'm going to piss meself again. I'm going to have a heart attack before I set foot in Teneriffe. Give us, give us, give us.

He removes all valuables from SAMMY *and puts them in his leather overcoat pockets.* AL *leads* SAMMY *off. A door bangs and sound of screams and a lavatory cistern.* AL *returns, tugging down his sleeves.*

AL: Well, we go and lay out the law then for the alibi?

RONNIE: Al, I've got five grands worth of sparklers tickling under me armpits. He didn't find all of it, thank Christ.

AL: More still there, good.

RONNIE: Got a Rennie? For me heart-burn.

AL: Nar.

RONNIE: We'd better get out of here.

AL: Yeah.

RONNIE: Dump this little lot of Sammy's somewhere.

AL: The sandpit?

RONNIE: Nar, somewhere less obvious Somewhere more safe . . . like –

AL: Like?

RONNIE: Somewhere where no-one would think of looking. Pam's old mum.

AL: What about her?

RONNIE: Her old lady, she's in hospital, right?

AL: Right.

RONNIE: Stuff the jewellery on her. I mean, the old Bill'd never think of looking for knocked off gear on some old cow dying in hospital, right.

AL: Nar. You're a genius Ronnie, a genius.

RONNIE: Then, when the heat's died off, collect the gear off her. Very safe deposit box, that old lady.

AL: Ronnie, without you, I'd only be half the man I am without you.

RONNIE: Let's shoot up the hospital.

A great roar from crowd off.

AL: That a goal?

RONNIE: Two goals in one match? This can't be West Ham . . .

They run off as Blackout.
Lights up on HENRY *and* EDNA's *room.* HENRY *leads on* ALBERT. HENRY *wears a party hat and apron;*

he is pouring wine. ALBERT *wears his Santa Claus suit and carries a sack of presents.* ALBERT *sits,* HENRY *hands him a glass.*

HENRY: Well? What do you think?

ALBERT: Not a great vino man, Henry, not a vino man. I've never been convinced those damned Froggies would go to all the trouble of getting out of the vat when they're tramping the grapes to go for a piss.

HENRY: Albert, really! Aren't you going to behave yourself?

ALBERT: I thought the only reason you invited me was in the hope that I wouldn't.

HENRY: R . . . r . . . really.

ALBERT: You really must do something about that infernal stutter Henry. You'll never get on *Call My Bluff.*

HENRY: Patrick C . . . C . . . Campbell.

ALBERT: Mind you, the Liberals seem to hog it. I hear the last time there was a three line whip, the BBC had to cancel the show.

HENRY (*sipping wine*): Mmm.

ALBERT: No spitting in the tram.

HENRY: Pardon?

ALBERT: Old notice, on the trams and trolley-buses. No spitting. If you're going to gob, just gob, I say.

HENRY: Fine bouquet.

ALBERT: Not a bad drop of plonk.

HENRY: You're very honoured. Only five bottles left. On my 21st birthday, my father laid down two dozen bottles.

ALBERT: On my 21st birthday, my father laid the barmaid at the Princess Alice. Family scandal. He was a character. A drayman for the brewery. You and he . . . (*Pause.*) I don't think you two would have gotten on.

Enter EDNA *with party hat.*

EDNA: Albert darling! Here's your party hat.

ALBERT: Happy Christmas, Edna. Nice of you to ask me. I say, this is all jolly festive. Even Bubbles there looks happy.

HENRY: I . . . I . . . I . . . (*He takes off his Pears Soap apron.*)

EDNA: I must say you've been quiet lately, Albert. I miss reading about you in the Evening Standard.

ALBERT: They got off me back when Harold kicked me into the Lords. Into the ermine truss and stuffed a chamber pot on me barnet.

EDNA: You always used to seem to be falling out of taxis and touching up the American ambassador and farting at Mrs Thatcher –

ALBERT: I know the Tories have been blown even further to the right lately but I can't claim full responsibility.

He hands them wrapped presents from his sack.

HENRY: I say Albert, that's jolly kind of you. You shouldn't have gone to all this trouble.

ALBERT: They're left-overs from the Great Ormond Street party. I've no idea what they might be.

The open the presents: an Actionman for HENRY, *a false beard and glasses for* EDNA.

EDNA: And for you Albert. (*Hands him a bottle of Chivas Regal. He has a party hat on now.*)

ALBERT: What's her name?

EDNA: Who?

ALBERT: And her fellow – what do you call him?

EDNA: O, Joan and Peter.

ALBERT: The kid, my young guest . . .

EDNA: Where is he?

HENRY: In the loo. Upset stomach.

ALBERT: And toothache. Got this damned toothache. Is the dentist bloke coming?

EDNA: Yes, yes. Joan's collecting him from the station in the next half an hour.

ALBERT: Good. Have a look at the kid.

EDNA: What's he like?

ALBERT: Seems . . . pretty ordinary. Some little problem or other, but he seems a bit shy about it.

EDNA: We thought it would be so nice to share a real old fashioned Christmas. You do think it's a good idea, don't you Albert?

ALBERT: I wouldn't say no to another G and T.

HENRY: You haven't had a G and T.

ALBERT: Then it's about bloody time I did. Large glass Henry.

EDNA: I wrapped up a present for the child. One of Adam's favourite old toys. Do you suppose he is all right? He seems to have been up there an awfully long time.

ALBERT: My fault. I fear I plied him with a little too much hospitality. Forget how kids vomit on the booze . . .

BUDDY *stands there.*

BUDDY: Here I stand, broken hearted. Spent a penny and only farted.

Pause.

Funny shaped bog. I couldn't find the chain.

HENRY: Ah, the bidet . . .

EDNA: O. I had anticipated someone a little younger. O do come in, do. We're so delighted you accepted our invitation. Do sit down, do. Or just wander freely if you like. Whatever you'd prefer to do. Just treat the place like home, after all, you're our guest. Adam –

HENRY: Our son –

EDNA: He was just about your age, when he was younger.

HENRY: My wife means –

EDNA: Adam used to spend an awful lot of time just lying on the floor picking his toenails so I mean, really, you treat the place like home.

BUDDY (*to* ALBERT, *whom he sits beside*): What's she going on about?

ALBERT: Let's all have a drink I say.

HENRY: OK old chap. Good to meet you. Any friend of Lord Plaistow's is a friend of ours. Just relax, you know. We're all pretty relaxed and free and easy here. Just spend Christmas in the way we usually spend the f . . . f . . . festive season.

EDNA (*sits beside* BUDDY): Adam would adore your safety pins.

BUDDY: What?

EDNA: Around your trousers.

BUDDY: To hold them up.

EDNA: Adam's got one in his nose.

BUDDY: Must be fucking long trousers.

Pause.

HENRY: I beg your pardon.

BUDDY: If he clips his trousers up to his nose.

EDNA: I meant – punk.

HENRY: I meant your language. There are no house rules here, but I mean, after all, it is Christmas.

ALBERT: Behave lads. No cussing in front of the ladies. Edna here, she's a lady.

EDNA: We've got a present for you.

BUDDY: Eh?

EDNA: A present for you.

BUDDY: For me?

EDNA: Yes.

BUDDY: What did you get a present for me for?

EDNA: Because it's Christmas.

BUDDY: I ain't got nothing for you.

EDNA: O, that doesn't matter. One doesn't give in the expectation of getting something in return. One gives simply for the pleasure of giving.

BUDDY: I did have a duck, but I give it to me Auntie Connie.

HENRY: I doubt she'll cook it as I'm cooking the duck tonight.

EDNA: I didn't realise you had a family. I thought you'd be an orphan at least.

BUDDY: Everyone's got a family.

EDNA: Yes, but –

ALBERT: The old drinks seem to be getting a little cold, Henry. Old Chubby Chops here hasn't had one yet.

HENRY: Ah yes, what would you like?

BUDDY: Drunk a lot already. Lord Plaistow, he kept topping me up when I weren't looking. So he could have a grope in the cab.

ALBERT *laughs and gropes him.* HENRY *pours* BUDDY *a beer.*

EDNA: Open the present then. And a party hat, you're not wearing a party hat.

She puts party hat on BUDDY's *head while he opens the present. A meccano set.*

BUDDY: O, lovely. Right what I needed.

HENRY: Cheers.

EDNA: Happy Christmas.

BUDDY: Ain't Christmas yet.

HENRY: Well, this is our Christmas. You see, we shall be away at Christmas.

EDNA: A fact-finding tour to the West Indies.

BUDDY: O.

EDNA: Your face looks terribly swollen.

BUDDY: Tooth hurting.

HENRY: Toothache can be ex . . . ex . . . ex . . .

EDNA: Excruciating.

HENRY: Extremely painful. Remember I had it at the by-election. What with the dashing about, it was days before I got it treated.

EDNA: I had toothache in Saudi Arabia one year.

ALBERT: I've never been on one of those fag-finding trips.

HENRY: Albert really! (*Laughs.*)

ALBERT: Not bugged, are we?

BUDDY: Me Auntie Connie . . .

Pause.

ALBERT: Your Auntie Connie?

BUDDY: This'll make you laugh. She had this bad tooth and she went to this dentist and he said: 'That's bad, got to come out.' Then he says: 'Blimey, here's another one what ought to come out' and then 'Christ, here's another one that ought to be extracted' and he says to her 'It's your decision like, what do you reckon?' And me Auntie Connie, she says: 'Sod it, take them all out' and when she come round after the gas, she never had a tooth left in her head. He'd taken *all* her teeth out and she only meant the three bad 'uns. What a laugh! She was right worried about what Uncle Harold was going to say. 'Cause he always reckoned she was bit of a daft old cow and she didn't much like him thinking she was a nutter, stands to reason, so he was meeting her outside the dentist's, like in the park and he had the Thermos with him and some cheese and pickle rolls and he says to her: 'Got your favourites, crusty ones!'

They all laugh.

She threw up over him. (*Pause, he stands.*) This was before they moved, into the country. Suffolk. Lovely there. The smell of the hay burning in the fields. Country smells. Breathe in the good country smells and you don't get in no more trouble, he said. Smell the country in this room. And flowers. Roses at Christmas?

EDNA (*shows him the roses in the bowl*): In October, the second bloom. Every year I cut a dozen roses and put them in the deep freeze and then thaw them just before Christmas. Yes, the roses do smell beautiful.

BUDDY: Can even cut flowers and freeze them? Freeze the smell of a rose? Breathe in the smell of the goodness and you won't get into any more trouble, he said.

HENRY: I've rather lost you, I'm afraid.

BUDDY: O . . . Me Uncle Harold said . . . the country, good things, London, he said, London – it's over.

HENRY: That could be Albert talking –

ALBERT: I spent a lifetime speaking; street corners, outside the dock gates, in the House. Words have no force, you know. To change things. He's the man your Uncle should thank. He's in the misgovernment.

HENRY: That kind of emotional Socialism is dead Albert. Lansbury's dead, Nye's dead –

BUDDY: Marc Bolan's dead.

ALBERT: Bloody Socialism's dead. Made extinct by his brand of government by accountancy. And, God help us, East London's dead.

HENRY: I agree I haven't held a seat there for quite as long as you Albert, but –

ALBERT: Dockland without the docks! Two decades ago, an impossibility.

HENRY: Newer industry, better housing. Anyway, the docks is only some emotional symbol. They were destined for the knackers' yard anyway in London, what with the larger vessels, containerisation –

ALBERT: Bollocks.

EDNA: Albert, you mustn't swear wearing a party hat.

ALBERT: Old Chubby Chops and me . . . (*Helps himself to another drink.*) We passed through what used to be the docklands in the Minicab. Took the road by the river, to here, Hornchurch. People down there, they're treated like driftwood. Places, didn't hardly recognise. Not a tinkle of a piano, not a throb of the old lifeblood. Memories bubbling about. I don't know whether it was the alcohol or flashes of genuine inspiration. Memories. New Years' Eves. Teeming with life. Childhood, adolescence, before the war, in the bitter winter afterwards. And every New Year's Eve, the ritual afterwards; just before midnight, we'd all take our glasses out into the backyard and see in the New Year. We'd stand out there in the dark and the frost, all the backyards full of neighbours. A hush. Looking towards the docks. The darkness pinpricked with coloured lights, along the funnels and the rigging of the vessels, outlining the cranes and running the lengths of the warehouse roofs. And at midnight, all the vessels from the seven oceans would sound their horns. Could hear them the entire length of the waterfront. Hundreds, hundreds. Giant, metallic choir. This year, there won't be a sound. Three vessels we counted, didn't we Chubby? Three vessels. God dammit, Hitler made the London docks his prime target at the height of the Blitz. Smash the London docks and you've smashed London. Night after night, we'd come out of the shelter; docks blazing, sky a brilliant carrot red. Kept the docks open, kept England's artery pumping. Our own legislators know how to do it. Simple. Rubber stamp.

HENRY: O Albert. Times pass, things change.

ALBERT: Nothing wrong is keeping the past as a lodestar.

HENRY: An uncle of mine, he did fire watching there you know. During the war. He says he'll never forget the night a German airman landed in the backyard of a pub. As though he'd just dropped in for a quick one. (*Laughs.*) They gave him a pint before they handed him over. He thought he was going to be lynched. His face. Docks blazing and – my uncle always says, his face – the hospitality. He says, that moment he knew we'd win the war.

ALBERT: That's the difference between us Henry. My lot was out fighting Hitler's mob and your lot was buying them fucking drinks.

EDNA: You're both boring our little guest. Henry, the dinner –

HENRY: Ah.

ALBERT: Everything's up to auction, to the highest bidder.

HENRY: Albert, you had the chance right after the war to create the ideal. Homes for heroes! New industries for a deprived area. You let the chance go begging –

EDNA: Now stop! You're boring our young friend.

BUDDY: I don't know what no-one's talking about.

HENRY: He's been bored to distraction by Albert's morbid memories. The good Lord Plaistow. Heavy booted man of the people.

ALBERT: Until they kicked me upstairs and –

HENRY:] Into the ermine truss and
ALBERT:] stuck a chamber pot on me barnet

HENRY: And avoided a scandal.

ALBERT: O, if it's to avoid scandals, they'd better build an extension to the House of Lords and let out the Commons as a dormitory for Japanese tourists.

HENRY: O come, I think there's quite enough hotel room. I mean, you should know far better than I. You sat on the board of one of the property companies that did so much of the building work in the beloved home-land.

ALBERT: I was defending the people I care for, safeguarding their interests.

HENRY: O, quite.

ALBERT: My intention in accepting the directorship was to ensure that they constructed as many cubic feet of homes as hotel space and yachting marinas.

HENRY: Pretty bloody unsuccessfully.

ALBERT: I never understood what those city slickers were talking about.

HENRY: You did very well for yourself out of the proceeds. Grand apartment in Westminster. Ideal Home magazine material.

ALBERT: Comfort for me old age. God dammit, I gave the best years of me life for peanuts.

HENRY: You're just a hypocrite, Albert.

ALBERT: At least my intentions were honourable.

HENRY: That's no defence.

ALBERT: And what about you Henry? What's this, your latest winter holiday jaunt? Jamaica again? Another fact-finding tour? Three winter holidays you've had there at the expense of the Jamaican government promising them you'll do a new deal to re-balance the sell-out for their sugar industry for the EEC. All it is is yet another free perk.

EDNA: I absolutely insist you two stop talking politics. It's so dreadfully boring. It's all argument and shouting. And the ridiculous truism is – you'll never alter each others opinions. It all depends on your point of view.

BUDDY: Eh?

EDNA: I said, it all depends on your point of view.

BUDDY: See! That's it. What I want someone to do.

EDNA: What?

BUDDY: Like someone who's good at talking and arguing an' that. Like, that's why I come to you Lord Plaistow. 'Cause Sammy said you could help.

ALBERT: How?

BUDDY: Explain to them. That it was an accident.

HENRY: What was?

BUDDY: What I done.

EDNA: What do you mean?

BUDDY: Like, well. The way you two were going at it like hammer and tongs, but you both reckon some of the things you done sounds a bit wrong if you don't get the chance to explain how it happened. (*Pause.*) Well, like, see . . . if you'd just explain to the governor . . . it was an accident.

HENRY: What was?

BUDDY: What I done.

EDNA: What do you mean?

BUDDY: This afternoon . . . how I spiked this screw. It weren't really a murder. I'm in a bit of a fix. And this fucking toothache. If I get this fixed, everything'll be all right, won't it . . .

Pause, then Blackout.
Radio message from police.
Back projection of exterior hospital, night, deserted street. A Christmas tree lit up outside.
Spotlight on PAM, *standing with a suitcase.*

PAM (*to audience*): They told me to bring her case of things. They phoned up. I thought they meant she was coming home, for Christmas. But I was a bit muddled with the Mogadons. When I eventually got here, she was gone. They'd transferred her. To Birmingham. For the blood. They'd rushed her up to Birmingham before I got the chance to get here.
What a night, eh, what a night? When I heard the phone, I thought it was in a dream. It was so vivid. I thought the phone was ringing in Teneriffe. I've seen the brochures of the apartments. I showed them to mum. She said: 'Nice.' She was very taken. She could have come and stayed. Not in the summer, 'cause she don't like the heat, see. But in the winter, for a bit of winter sunshine. We would have had our Christmas dinner on the patio. I don't know about a roast, but something nice, not oily. Sitting on the patio looking out at the sea with the palm trees making shadows in the sunshine. With mum and Buddy. Buddy. And after dinner we'd have all gone down to the pool for a swim. See, there's this pool on this estate we had in mind in Teneriffe. You only have to pay £3 a month for full access; all the apartments' residents can use it, for £3 a month. The lady in the greengrocers told me. And I thought perhaps Buddy could get a job out there, on the estate. Away from all the bad influences. Know what I mean? And I was swimming and I got out of the pool and mum was sitting there under a sunshade at a table beside the pool and she was knitting this little white baby suit and I said: 'Mum, what are you making?' and she just smiled and I knew, knew it was for me baby. (*Pause.*) That's why I didn't hear the door. I was so asleep. The Old Bill, they just smashed it down and come in and took away all the stuff. All the teles and the coats and the stereos and . . . everything. When they find Ronnie! That's it, as far as I'm concerned. And when they find Buddy . . . When they find him . . .

Enter RONNIE *and* AL.

RONNIE: Pam.

PAM: What are you doing here?

RONNIE: At the flats, nosey old cow next door, she said you'd shot down to the hospital here.

PAM: I brought mum's things. I thought she was coming home for Christmas.

RONNIE: Coming home?

PAM: No.

AL: I hate the smell of hospitals. Makes me feel ill.

RONNIE: Listen Pam, so Old Bill cleared out all the gear then?

PAM *begins to cry.*

AL: Ronnie, she's crying.

RONNIE: Hang about, hang about. For Christ's sake, Pam. This is important.

PAM: Ronnie, I don't know why I don't hate you.

RONNIE: Pam, don't get sentimental.

PAM: You're a bastard, a right bastard.

AL: Ronnie, do you reckon she's all right?

RONNIE: Listen, Pam. A couple of hours ago we unloaded a few grands worth of sparklers on your mum.

PAM: They've transferred her, to the Birmingham blood centre.

RONNIE: Fantastic ruby necklace, must be worth five grand. And rings and –

PAM: I think she must be worse.

AL: Who must be?

PAM: Me mum.

RONNIE: Sorry about that.

PAM: It's the shame you've brought on the family. That's what's made her worse.

RONNIE: Don't say that. You don't know what you're talking about. She's a bit upset.

AL: She looks a bit upset.

PAM: I am upset. She's been transferred.

RONNIE: When?

PAM: Just before I got here. I brought her case and –

RONNIE: Jesus Christ! She looked as right as rain a couple of hours ago when I stuffed her the jewellery. She said it was the nicest Christmas present she'd ever had.

PAM: It was seeing you that made her relapse.

RONNIE: Listen Pam, you'd better have a word with the matron. See if they took the stuff off her before the transfer.

AL (*slowly realising*): If they've transferred her to Birmingham . . . say she's still got the jewellery?

RONNIE: Al, will you excuse us a moment. I must comfort my wife in her moment of distress.

AL: Eh?

RONNIE: Fuck off.

AL: O. I'll be outside.

AL *exits. Pause.*

RONNIE: Pam, I want you to go and see the matron. They might have taken the sparklers off her and bungled them in a safe or . . . Pam, I'm doing the decent thing. I'm telling you that Al and me are going to piss off for a bit, till the heat dies off. We need them jewels now to pay for the hideout.

PAM: Serves you right. It's all over Ronnie. I don't want this life no more. You've contaminated me. Like you've contaminated Buddy, poor Buddy. I've had enough of being married to a villain.

RONNIE: Sure, sure – but just this last favour.

PAM: No.

RONNIE: Pam.

She spits in his face. He hits her. Pause.

RONNIE: Sorry love, I didn't mean, I . . .

She holds her eye. AL *enters.*

AL: She all right?

RONNIE: Bitch, stupid fucking bitch. Let's get to that fucking sand-pit.

RONNIE *and* AL *exit. Blackout. Police message.*
Harsh dentist surgery lights up on ALBERT *with a bottle and still in his Santa Claus clothes and* HENRY, *in a fur overcoat.* BUDDY *is half asleep in the dentist's chair.*

ALBERT: Well?

HENRY: He's on his way.

ALBERT: About time.

HENRY: If word of this leaks out . . . it doesn't bear thinking about.

ALBERT: Doesn't it?

HENRY: I had to give Edna a tranquilliser. The press are going to love this, aren't they. 'Government Minister entertains on the run murderer to Christmas dinner.'

ALBERT: In times of crisis, remember what Churchill said.

HENRY: What?

ALBERT: I don't mind if I do. (*Takes a hefty swig from the bottle.*)

BUDDY *groans, his eyes still closed.*

God, get a move on Peter, get a move on. (*To* BUDDY.) You'll be all right, lad. Dentist on his way. He'll send you to sleep.

HENRY: Yes, Albert'll recite you one o his speeches.

ALBERT: The dentist'll know what to

do. Treat you. You stuck a frozen eel up her nose. Have you phoned the police Henry.

HENRY: Not ex . . ex . . exactly. My intention is to. But I was just p . . . p . . . pondering on what might be the best way of going about it.

ALBERT: How do you mean?

HENRY: You see, we're both somewhat compromised. I mean, if the press get hold of this! Just see the headlines. Minister entertains . . . it doesn't bear thinking about.

ALBERT: I hadn't thought of that.

HENRY: Then it's about fucking time you did. Look, what I propose is . . . we anaesthetise what's his name here, treat him, and whilst he's comatose, transport him back to your flat, and then you telephone the police and tell them he's been in your flat all the time.

ALBERT: And mysteriously had a tooth extracted.

HENRY: No. You phoned Peter and Peter went to your flat and did it. Code of ethics. He couldn't refuse to treat someone in pain.

ALBERT: Now wait a minute. So when the shit hits the fan, it goes straight into my face?

HENRY: But Albert, you've had so little publicity lately. People will begin to think you're dead. You're infamous – I mean, legendary for helping kids in trouble.

ALBERT: Don't be stupid. The kid'll tell them right away he was at your house.

HENRY: No, he was delirious with pain. And the story'll do wonders for your memoirs. Newspaper serialisations be worth a few thousand pounds. It can only benefit you.

ALBERT: You may be right Henry. If I say –

BUDDY: Oi! You fucking bastards.

ALBERT: OK Chubby, let's calm down –

BUDDY: Don't you talk to me, you pouffy bastard. Heard you. Heard you. Your plans. To get out. Get out of the embarrassment. That I caused you lot.

ALBERT: Not me.

BUDDY: Going to make money out of me. Sell the story to the papers. You get rich out of what I done. I spent all night. I was so frightened. You ever been so frightened you think you're going to die? Die of fright? Talked to people, heard stories . . . legends . . . old fighter . . . villains . . . priest cheated me . . . All I wanted all the time was the chance to . . . explain . . . hospital, me mum dying . . . her life . . . nothing – seen other lives, rich lives –

ALBERT: I slaved a lifetime to make more lives better.

BUDDY: Ain't done much fucking good have you. All the kids inside, I mean . . . kids where I just come from, what they done seems a bit fucking pathetic compared to what you posh lot have done. Snotty drawers and her car fiddle. Only it's legal. But your Jamaican trip, that ain't is it Henry.

HENRY: Perfectly acceptable practice.

BUDDY: Come off it.

ALBERT: Actually, it's quite above board.

BUDDY: What about your property company director lark?

ALBERT: Not illegal, not illegal.

BUDDY: It must be.

ALBERT: No.

BUDDY: Can't be right.

ALBERT: Absolutely right.

BUDDY: Making money out of me?

ALBERT: I haven't done anything of the sort –

BUDDY: Yet. You will. Your riches, all comes from other peoples' pain.

Enter JOAN *in a fur coat.*

ALBERT: I thought you'd gone to get Peter.

JOAN: I'm not helping that vicious little shit. As far as I'm concerned, the police can chop off his bollocks with a rusty fret-saw.

HENRY: Joan –

JOAN: His photo's in the Evening Standard. Nationwide manhunt. Hanging's too good for the likes of him. And he stole £500 from my purse.

BUDDY: Five hundred? (*Laughs, slurps.*)

JOAN: Have you called the police?

HENRY: We were just discussing the right approach.

JOAN: There's only one. Pick up the phone and dial.

PETER *enters. In a white dentist's coat.*

ALBERT: Ah, there you are Peter –

HENRY: Peter, perhaps you could restrain your wife before we've had the chance to –

PETER (*to* BUDDY): Open your mouth let's have a look.

Takes the dentistry mirror and a tool from the table of instruments beside the chair.

JOAN: Use an axe.

HENRY: You understand, our problem is basically that –

PETER: Please get out of my surgery.

HENRY: But we must decide –

JOAN: I shall call the murder squad.

PETER: Will you please leave my surgery and do your decision making some other place.

JOAN: He's a murderer!

PETER: I'm a dentist. Go on, please.

ALBERT, HENRY *and* JOAN *exit.* PETER *examines* BUDDY's *open mouth.*

PETER: Ah, I see . . .

He takes the tweezers and removes a small temporary filling from a tooth cavity.

This wasn't much good.

BUDDY: I put it in. To try and stop it hurting. It still hurt though.

PETER: Now let's see. See what the trouble is. Cavity. Filling came out, a deep one and . . . this'll hurt.

BUDDY *yells.* PETER *removes a tiny piece of silver paper from* BUDDY's *tooth.*

Silver paper. Chocolate on it. You should take the foil off before you eat it. Caught in the cavity.

BUDDY: The village poufs. They brought in some chocolate before the match, for us. We don't get it much.

PETER: What match?

BUDDY: Football match. Prestige match with the village.

PETER: Tried to bribe you, did they?

BUDDY: Eh?

PETER: To lose the game?

BUDDY: O. It don't hurt now.

PETER: Silver paper touching the nerve. Bet it did hurt. Needs a new filling.

BUDDY: Another time. Just wanted the pain to stop. Clear me head of the pain. Clearer now. Thank you.

PETER: What?

BUDDY: For helping me.

PETER: It's my job.

BUDDY: Know what I done?

PETER: Yes, I heard.

BUDDY: Don't you . . . hate me?

PETER: Hate you?

BUDDY: Everyone, when they saw me, heard what I done. They went berserk. Like I was the plague or something.

PETER: Well, some people, they over-react.

BUDDY: You remind me of the priest. So calm. So . . . calm. So peaceful. Relaxing. Then he betrayed me, sounded the alarm.

PETER: I suppose he thought he was doing what he should do.

BUDDY: Bit generous, aren't you?

PETER: Why not be? There's enough who aren't.

BUDDY: I don't understand you. I gave your missus the shits.

PETER: Yes. (*Brief laugh.*) She told me.

BUDDY: Don't you want revenge? To punish me like?

PETER: I think there's enough who want to punish. I don't feel any inherent need to . . . pay-back.

BUDDY: You're kind.

PETER: Kind?

BUDDY: The screw, he was kind.

PETER: Are you going to stab me?

BUDDY (*takes a syringe from the table*): I could – with this needle.

PETER: Maybe.

BUDDY: Aren't you frightened?

PETER: I don't think you want to stab anyone.

BUDDY: I didn't want to make him die.

PETER: Accident?

BUDDY: Accident, yeah.

PETER: Would you like someone to speak for you? Perhaps I could help you . . . explain. To them. To the governor.

BUDDY: Who?

PETER: Me.

Silence.

BUDDY (*giggles*): All night . . . all night . . . I've been looking . . . looking for someone to do that.

PETER: Well?

BUDDY: Bit late now. Too late. Now it's too late.

PETER: It's never too late.

BUDDY: The time has passed when it could work.

PETER: Well. You can't run away for ever.

BUDDY: So?

PETER: I'll have to tell them.

BUDDY: Yeah?

PETER: It's my duty. To phone the police.

BUDDY: I could do a bunk, out the fire exit there . . . while you're on the phone.

PETER: You said it yourself. Every hour's delay in going back makes it worse. I shall phone the police now.

PETER *exits.* BUDDY *takes the screw's whistle from his pocket and fingers it as the lights begin to fade. Enormous back projection of the empty docks at night. One vessel amid the cranes. A ship's horn sounds. The snow begins to fall.*
Darkness, just the back projection. Lights up, still snowing.
The sandpit snow covered and the tractor tyre swing.
Another foghorn sounds as RONNIE *and* AL *enter hurriedly with torches and two leather grips. They go to the sandpit.*

RONNIE: Right, here we go, then catch that plane.

AL: Have to get our skates on. Should have gone to Birmingham first and got the jewels off the old cow. What a waste.

RONNIE: Enough here. Let's dig it up.

AL: I've never been to Teneriffe Ronnie.

RONNIE: Good old Frank. There's a real mate. Time of crisis, one phone call and he's got us two airline tickets. Class. No Panic Frank. Flights on the first plane. Just get up the rest of this gear and, away.

AL: Six thousand pounds.

RONNIE: Easy. I phoned Larry the Elbows. He's got the readies to buy the gear. Very organised, salvage job but –

AL: Very organised.

RONNIE: You have to be nowadays. No more coshing milkman. Bit of class. There'll be a lot of redevelopment here now they've closed the docks. Posh area, it'll be. Make a fortune we shall. There's a lot of fucking money about.

AL: I just hope no-one's looking.

RONNIE: Relax Al. For Christ's sake relax. It's snowing. Foggy. No-one up there in the flats'll be able to see us.

AL: It's cold enough to freeze your bollocks off tonight. I'll keep a look out.

He goes to flash the torch off.

RONNIE: Three paces from the edge . . . (*Measures the spot in the sandpit.*)

AL: I'm freezing to death.

RONNIE: This time tomorrow you'll be sunbathing.

AL: Hey!

PAM *enters. She has a black eye.* AL *shines the torch on her face.*

PAM: It's only me.

RONNIE: What the bloody hell you doing here? I told you to piss off you cow. I never want to see you again in all my life.

PAM: I know. You told me when you split my eyeball.

RONNIE: Lost me temper.

PAM: You always have been impetuous.

RONNIE: Clear off, will you.

PAM: Frank rang, Frank from Heathrow. He said it's snowing.

RONNIE: I know it's fucking snowing.

AL: I know it's snowing.

PAM: He said the flight's been cancelled. The flight to Teneriffe, because of the snow. I never knew you was doing a bunk to Teneriffe. Ronnie, that news hurt me more than when you hit me. That was our dream. Ours.

RONNIE: Yeah, well. That's the way it goes.

PAM: Anyway, the flight's cancelled. You can't go tonight. I just thought I'd tell you. To save you a wasted journey.

AL: Fuck it.

PAM: I'll miss you Ronnie, in a funny way. Thing's will seem boring without you. Without a villain. Nice and better but . . . a bit boring.

She goes. AL *and* RONNIE *stare at each other.*

AL: What'll we do then?

RONNIE: Christ. Bloody women.

AL: That's why I never got married, Ronnie. Never settled down. Me mum put me off the idea.

RONNIE: What'll we do? Go to Heathrow. In the next bar. Till there is a flight. Heathrow, here we come.

AL: Yeah.

RONNIE: Fucking Ada. I don't believe it.

AL: Get a move on Ronnie, I'm getting nervous.

RONNIE: Jesus, the bastard. The bastard. It's all frozen. It's all frozen over, like an ice rink.

AL: What are you talking about Ronnie?

RONNIE: All this fucking sleet, the cold. It's settled on the sandpit and frozen over. It's all frozen.

AL: But Ronnie – all the sparklers we nicked are buried under there.

RONNIE: Now tell me something I don't know.

AL: Mind you don't piss your pants again Ronnie.

RONNIE: Got a Rennie? Heartburn.

AL: Here. (*Hands him a packet.*) Got them from the nurses in the hospital.

RONNIE: Jesus.

AL: Crack open the ice. With a . . . with a . . . If only I hadn't dumped that fucking iron bar.

RONNIE: Need a pick axe or a . . .

AL: I ain't got a pick axe handy. Jump on it, smash it. Must smash the ice.

AL *and* RONNIE *jump up and down on the ice. They jump wildly, screaming. Then they tire. They stand breathing heavily.*

BUDDY *has entered. He wears a long black leather overcoat. He watches them grinning.*

BUDDY: Pathetic.

RONNIE *is embarrassed by* BUDDY's *presence. He turns his back on* BUDDY *and speaks quickly to* AL.

AL: Thousands under here.

RONNIE: It's fucked, it's a blow out, we've had it. The best night's work I've ever done. Let's find Bert and Ginger Jug Ears and find a card school. Come back and get it tomorrow.

AL: It'll have melted tomorrow.

RONNIE: Fucking better have.

They exit hurriedly. BUDDY *laughs. Sound of* SAMMY *approaching singing 'Goodbyee'.*
SAMMY *enters, then is suddenly aware of* BUDDY *in the shadows.*

SAMMY: Go on mug me, whoever you are. Mug me up. Kill me.

He turns to see BUDDY.

SAMMY: I took it, but they took it back.

BUDDY: There's more buried down there. But it's all frozen over. They can't get at it.

SAMMY: There's more? I never found it all? (*Laughs.*) You look like Ronnie.

BUDDY: Ronnie? He's small time.

SAMMY: The coat –

BUDDY: Nicked it from a motor.

Pause. Fog horn from docks.

SAMMY: What'll you do boy? You can't run away for ever. Once the docks was the place runaways went. Biggest docks in the world at one time. Miles and miles of ships. To far-away places. Stowaway on a ship. Hardly see a ship there now. There's one this tonight. It's all over here. London, East London – it's smashed. You and me, we're the casualties of the peace. There was a time they respected an honest fighting man. Time was they respected a villain. All that's gone.

BUDDY: Docks gone. Houses gone. Can't kill the people.

SAMMY: They've had a bloody good try.

BUDDY: Take away the night you won your title?

SAMMY: Never take away the night I won me title.

BUDDY: Once a fighter?

SAMMY: Always a fighter.

BUDDY: Keep fighting?

SAMMY: Keep fighting.

BUDDY: What with?

SAMMY: Need money?

BUDDY: I give mine to you.

SAMMY: I'll give you better than money boy. (*Takes a necklace from his pocket.*) Ronnie never got this. I had it down me pants keeping me balls warm. Here, take it.

BUDDY: What's the use of this to me, what I've done?

SAMMY: Flog it. Face, swellng's gone down.

BUDDY: Dentist fixed it. One of Lord Plaistow's friends.

SAMMY: He helped?

BUDDY: He's a villain.

SAMMY: He is.

BUDDY: Yeah, he's a villain.

Another fog horn from a ship.

SAMMY: Getting read to sail. Saw it, a Brazilian vessel. She'll never come back to the London docks.

BUDDY: I used to lay in bed on foggy nights, listening to the sound of the horns. Wondering where they was going to. Rio de Janeiro and Marseilles and Australia and New York and . . . How do you stowaway on a vessel then?

SAMMY: Easy. You walk on and then you hide. Like you've been doing ashore all night.

BUDDY: Yeah.

SAMMY: Need money for the bus – to get to the ship?

BUDDY: I nicked a Government Minister's motor.

SAMMY: Drive it in the river. They'll give him another one. Backhander.

BUDDY: Keep fighting?

SAMMY: You ain't evil, boy. I know you ain't evil.

BUDDY: What I done ain't nothing compared to what a lot of people I met have done.

SAMMY: I killed a man once, in the ring.

BUDDY: Lord Plaistow, he telled me.

SAMMY: Accident, scar for life.

BUDDY: Mine an accident and all.

SAMMY: Enough scars here. Desolation, all around. Want this? Be a tamed pigeon, boy? Never, not you, not me – we're fighters.

BUDDY: Stowaway? On the ship?

SAMMY: Take the necklace.

BUDDY: Man died under a frozen stream. His last message – 'Goodbye cruel world.'

SAMMY: There's another message. 'Fuck you cruel world.' I'd be an anarchist, but I can't spell it.

Another horn.

SAMMY: If you're going to go . . .

BUDDY: Yeah.

SAMMY: Go boy go.

BUDDY: If you see Pam –

SAMMY: Pam?

BUDDY: Ronnie's wife –

SAMMY: Ah?

BUDDY: Tell her, don't keep getting drunk.

SAMMY: Like me?

BUDDY *hesitates, then goes.* SAMMY *sits on the swing.*

SAMMY: In court one day I was . . . it was me anniversary, me hundredth appearance for being drunk and disorderly. The magistrate, an intelligent man, deeply intelligent – do-gooder – he said he'd give me one last chance. Said he wouldn't put me in the cells. Stupid bastard. He said drink was my problem. Brilliant man. He said if I promised never to drink again, if I kept off the booze, he said he'd let me off. He said I mustn't touch a drop, not a drop. Not, he said, not even a glass of sherry before dinner.

He laughs, swings, drinks from a bottle.

Be optimistic he said. Optimist. I sat on park swings in the twenties, thirties in the depression. I saw bare-footed kids running wild in the streets with rickets in their legs and scars of malnutrition. You ever wondered why the East End threw up so many light weights and fly weights? Skinny kids without an ounce of spare flesh. I see them. I see them in the slums and I say: I've seen deprivation and poverty and seen rats chewing babies in slum rooms. But I ain't a pessimist. Smash down the manor, rip it up, smash it down, fuck up decent peoples' lives but – the tribe lives on. Kid there. Never give in, never surrender. Do what the fuck you like to us mister. Can't destroy that heart. It's in the blood. Never kill that. Never. Bon voyage kiddo, bon voyage.

Horn sounds. Blackout.
Music loud: Boomtown Rats 'Joey's on the Street Again' from the album Boomtown Rats, Ensign label.

End of Play